The

INNOVATIVE
LEADER

The
INNOVATIVE
LEADER

How to inspire your team and drive creativity

PAUL SLOANE

KOGAN PAGE

London and Philadelphia

Publisher's note
Every possible effort has been made to ensure that the information contained in this book is accurate at the time of going to press, and the publishers and author cannot accept responsibility for any errors or omissions, however caused. No responsibility for loss or damage occasioned to any person acting, or refraining from action, as a result of the material in this publication can be accepted by the editor, the publisher or the author.

First published in Great Britain and the United States in 2007 by Kogan Page Limited

120 Pentonville Road
London N1 9JN
United Kingdom
www.kogan-page.co.uk

525 South 4th Street, #241
Philadelphia PA 19147
USA

© Paul Sloane, 2007

The right of Paul Sloane to be identified as the author of this work has been asserted by him in accordance with the Copyright, Designs and Patents Act 1988.

ISBN-10 0 7494 5001 0
ISBN-13 978 0 7494 5001 4

British Library Cataloguing-in-Publication Data

A CIP record for this book is available from the British Library.

Library of Congress Cataloging-in-Publication Data

Sloane, Paul, 1950-
    The innovative leader : how to inspire your team and drive creativity / Paul Sloane. p. cm.
    ISBN-13: 978-0-7494-5001-4
    ISBN-10: 0-7494-5001-0
    1. Creative ability in business. 2. Creative ability in business--Case studies. 3. Leadership. I. Title.
    HD53.S567 2007
    658.4'092--dc22
                                                                        2007001971

Typeset by Jean Cussons Typesetting, Diss, Norfolk
Printed and bound in Great Britain by Creative Print and Design (Wales), Ebbw Vale

Contents

About the author

Author and speaker on creative problem solving and lateral leadership

Paul Sloane is an entertaining, thought-provoking, motivational speaker and a recognized expert on innovation, lateral thinking and leadership. He is the author of 17 books on lateral puzzles, creative problem solving and lateral leadership. Over 2 million copies of his books have been sold. He was described in the *Independent* as the 'King of lateral thinking puzzles'. He is the founder of Destination-Innovation (www.destination-innovation.com), a consultancy that helps organizations improve innovation.

He facilitates meetings, leads workshops and gives after-dinner talks and keynote addresses. His talks offer a unique blend of puzzling challenges, humour and hard-hitting business messages. His workshops provide practical techniques to improve leadership and innovation. Clients include AA, American Express, ARM, BT, Cendant, DWP, HMRC, Home Office, Lloyds of London, OGC, Shell and 3M.

Paul took a first in Engineering at Cambridge. He joined IBM, where he came top of Sales School. He was part of the team that launched the IBM PC in the UK. He went on to be MD of the database leaders Ashton-Tate. He became VP International for MathSoft Inc. and CEO of Monactive Ltd.

In his book *The Leader's Guide to Lateral Thinking Skills* (2003), also published by Kogan Page, Paul explains how you can use the principles of lateral leadership to inspire your people to achieve breakthrough solutions and radical innovations. His articles on innovation and leadership have appeared in leading business publications. His inspirational talks on innovation, creative thinking and leadership, described as 'rocket fuel for the business brain', have proved popular with conference audiences in Europe, the United States, South Africa and Asia.

Introduction

The need for innovation is well understood. It is now common-place for leaders to stress the critical importance of creativity and innovation to the future of their organizations. Managers who believed that just doing the same things faster or cheaper would be sufficient for success (or even survival) now acknowledge that this approach is quite insufficient. If you keep doing the same things then competitors will overtake you. They will take your customers away from you in all sorts of inventive ways. In the government sector it is recognised that spending more money on problems is not enough. The demands are growing so fast that doing more of the same is no answer. New ways of doing things have to be found. New products, services, methods and partnerships are needed.

But this recognition leads to a host of questions. What sort of person is an innovative leader? What can the leader do? As a leader, how can you transform your people from cubicle dwellers into innovation warriors? Where can the ideas come from to fuel the supply of innovation? How can you turn your complacent organization into a powerhouse of invention and entrepreneurial achievement? Where will you find the time and resources to try new things when you are so busy running the current model? What can be done to overcome a culture that is risk averse? How can you replace a culture of comfortable incremental progress into one of hungry adventure?

This book was written to address these kinds of issues – and not in some grand theoretical framework but in the form of practical tips and methods that can be put into immediate effect. It is aimed at the person who wants to turn themselves and their team into commanders of creativity and maestros of innovation. There is advice for leaders to help them change their organizations, for managers who are charged with making innovation happen and for individuals who want to be more creative.

It is based on experiences and insights gained in working with business leaders and in running innovation workshops across the world. It is designed to be read in bite-sized chunks – easily digestible for busy executives who want to start a revolution in their business. This is no easy task, but help is at hand. Start biting and start the revolution.

Section 1:
Leading innovation

1. HAVE A VISION FOR CHANGE

You cannot expect your team to be innovative if they do not know the direction in which they are headed. Innovation has to have a purpose. It is up to the leader to set the course and give a bearing for the future. This is set in broad terms and is described as the mission, core purpose or vision for the organisation. Although each of these is different, they share much in common, and whichever you choose, there should be one overarching statement which defines the direction for the business and which people will readily understand and remember.

Jack Welch, ex-CEO of GE said, 'Good business leaders create a vision, articulate the vision, passionately own the vision, and relentlessly drive it to completion.'

Many mission statements are boring, long-winded, long on platitudes and short on inspiration. Here are some good ones:

Lego – To nurture the child in each of us.

Disney Corporation – To use our imagination to bring happiness to millions of people.

Merck – We are in the business of preserving and improving human life.

Tesco – To create value for customers to earn their lifetime loyalty.

The Home Office – A safe, just, tolerant society.

3M – To be the most innovative enterprise in the world.

WPP – To develop and manage talent; to apply that talent throughout the world for the benefit of clients; to do so in partnership; to do so for profit.

GlaxoSmithKline – To improve the quality of human life by enabling people to do more, feel better and live longer.

As a leader you don't want happy, comfortable people in your team. You want passionate, energetic people who are keen for the journey and ready to take on a challenge. Your job is to communicate a destination and to persuade them it is a target they can believe in and a goal worth reaching. You can then ask them how best to reach the destination. Once you have established a vision that is inspiring you can ask people to be creative and innovative in moving towards it.

The vision or mission is the starting point for strategic plans, objectives and metrics. The key performance indicators of the business will measure how progress is made in meeting the goals that flow from the vision. Striving for the vision will always involve change. It is a journey from where we are today to a better future. There is a risk in making the changes necessary on this journey but the leader has to persuade people that there is a bigger risk in standing still. The organizations that have no vision for the future and no desire to change are the ones destined for obscurity and obsolescence.

Just painting the picture is not enough. It quickly fades from view if it is not constantly reinforced. Great leaders spend time with their teams. They illustrate the vision, the goals and the challenges. They explain to people how their role is crucial in fulfilling the vision and meeting the challenges. They inspire men and women to become passionate entrepreneurs finding innovative routes to success.

2. ISSUE A DECLARATION OF INNOVATION

Many CEOs and leaders talk about the importance of innovation in their organizations. But often their words are bland and vague – just a form of management-speak. If you want people really to believe, then why not explain exactly what you mean with a declaration of innovation.

The declaration of innovation is a statement of commitment and intent. It should contain the following elements:

- An explanation of why innovation is critical for the organization.

- A list of some of the key areas where innovation is needed – launching new products or services, breaking into new markets, replacing processes with better ones, finding new ways to source materials, reducing costs, recruiting and motivating people, partnering and so on.

- A request for every employee to contribute his or her ideas.

- A commitment to listen and respond to all ideas.

- A commitment to allocate resources – in particular time, training and money – for creativity, idea development and innovation.

- An idea management and evaluation process.

- A determination to look for ideas from all sources, including outside the organization.

- An affirmation of a positive attitude towards risk and failure. In particular, a message that employees will not be criticized or blamed for honest innovative endeavours that do not succeed.

The declaration of innovation becomes a manifesto for change in the organization. It endorses the vision, culture and processes of innovation. It is made available to all employees. New starters get it as part of their documents of employment. It is available on the intranet. It is a powerful reminder to everyone that innovation is not just a buzzword; it is part of the DNA of the organization.

3. SET DRASTIC EXPECTATIONS

Most business leaders plan modest incremental growth each year. They set expectations they are confident can be achieved. This way everyone can get a pat on the back when the plan is reached. Growth in revenue in line with the market at 5 per cent and growth in profits of 6 per cent are the sort of results business leaders plan. Many directors would be delighted with such results.

The trouble with this approach is that it reinforces incrementalism. The easiest way to get 5 per cent growth is by pumping up the existing products or services. We can add some line extensions. The easiest way to wring out some extra profit is to improve the efficiency of the current model or to squeeze down on our suppliers. There is no incentive here to look for big opportunities, to find entirely new sources of revenue, to conceive new business models.

The second problem is that companies, just like children, tend to conform to the expectations set for them. If 5 per cent growth is considered a good result and 7 per cent is considered a demanding 'stretch' target, then few in company will believe that anything greater than 7 per cent is possible. Just like children who are constrained by their parents' lack of belief, the people in the business match their collective norms.

Outstanding companies set outstanding expectations. Businesses that want to break out of the pack demand more of themselves. This is what GE Capital says about expectations (quoted in Hamel, 2002: 254): 'It is expected that we will grow our earnings by 20% per year or more. When you have objectives that are outlandish it forces you to think differently about your opportunities. If one guy has a 10% target and another has a 20% target, the second guy is going to do different things.'

Drastic expectations reinforce the declaration of innovation and the innovation goals. If people realize that just doing what everyone else in the market is doing is not enough, then they will respond. Average expectations about the company encourage people to think and act averagely. Drastic expectations encourage people to think innovatively and act like entrepreneurs.

4. FIGHT THE FEAR OF CHANGE

People are naturally apprehensive about change. They fear the unknown. There is a reluctance to take risks. This can be particularly true in a successful enterprise. Success can be an enemy of innovation. Why mess with a model that works? There is little incentive to take risks and try new things. But even successful companies are at risk if they stand still. Polaroid Corporation was a leader in its field but digital camera technology dealt it a serious blow and pushed it into Chapter 11. Smith Corona was very successful making typewriters but the advent of word processors proved fatal to its business.

Overcoming the fear of change is a key objective for innovative leaders. They will need to take this issue head-on. They engage people in a dialogue and discuss the risks and benefits of standing still or of innovating. The types of messages they strive to convey are:

- We are doing well right now but we need to do better.

- We must fight the risk of complacency.

- If we don't find new ways to reach and delight our customers, then others will do it for us.

- There is a risk in innovating but there is a bigger risk in standing still.

- Change can be a big positive for us if we can drive it in the direction we want.

Here are some tools you can use in the battle to win the hearts and minds of your people:

- stories about companies that focused on what they did well and missed the next big wave;

- examples of how we lost business to more innovative competitors;

- examples of how we won business by doing something new;

- praise for risk takers and entrepreneurs within the business who have helped to drive change — successfully or unsuccessfully.

Above all you must promote a dialogue where, in addition to telling these messages, you listen to people's concerns and solicit their input. You can turn negative people around by asking for their views on how to make things better. When asked they will often volunteer great ideas for how we can make the change a big success.

Innovative leaders constantly evangelize the need for change. They replace the comfort of complacency with the hunger of ambition: 'We are doing well but we cannot rest on our laurels – we need to do even better.' They explain that while trying new ventures is risky, standing still is riskier. They must paint a picture that shows an appealing future worth taking risks to achieve. The prospect involves perils and opportunities. The only way we can get there is by embracing change.

5. TELL STORIES

If you want to persuade your people to join you on a challenging quest, then you cannot rely on a series of spreadsheets and Microsoft PowerPoint slides to do it. You want a response that is just as much emotional as rational. People relate to stories much more than they do to graphs, diagrams and percentages. You must appeal to their hearts as well as their brains.

What kinds of stories should you tell? It depends. Stories about the history of the company can help define the values you stand for. Stories about yourself, some of your learning experiences and mistakes that you made can help people understand what is important to you and your beliefs. Stories about employees who took risks or did exceptional things can inspire and motivate. Stories about how other companies failed or succeeded can show the dangers of complacency or the benefits of change. Each story should involve people who you describe so that your audience can relate to them and understand their feelings and motivations.

Anne Mulcahy took over as CEO of Xerox Corporation in 2001 when it was in serious trouble. She turned it around and sharply increased profits and the stock price. In an interview with Keith Hammond, published in *Fast Company* in March 2005, she says:

> Storytelling is hugely important. At our town meetings the most frequently asked questions were not whether we'd survive but what we would look like when we did. I got great advice; write a story. We wrote a Wall Street Journal style article dated five years out. It was about where we could be if we really stood up to the plate. People loved it. No matter where I go people pull that article out. They personalised it. Stories exist at all levels of the corporation. You talk to tech reps and they will tell you what they did to help turn this company around. Everyone has a story. That creates powerful momentum – people's sense that they can do good things. It's much more powerful than the precision of the strategy.

One December a copy-machine operator at Kinko's, a major chain of outlets providing copying and document services, noticed a customer struggling at the copy machine. Demand for copying is normally low in December because people are busy with Christmas. So the operator asked what the customer was doing. 'I am creating personalised calendars with family photos for each month as gifts,' was the reply. The operator thought this was an opportunity that could be developed so he phoned the founder and CEO of Kinko's, Paul Orfalea, and explained the idea. Orfalea was so excited by it that he rushed it out as a service in all outlets. It was very successful and a new product – custom calendars – and a new revenue stream were created.

The Kinko's story can be used to make various points – eg about empowerment, about communication or about how employees can see things that leaders can not.

As you read business books and magazines look out for stories you can use to illustrate your points. When you meet people inside the organization watch for personal stories that show the problems you face and how they can be overcome. Use these anecdotes when you communicate – people will remember them long after the corporate Microsoft PowerPoint slides are forgotten.

6. SET GOALS FOR INNOVATION

Most organizations recognize that innovation is critical for survival and success but very few know how to set goals or metrics for innovation. The most common target used is the percentage of revenues derived from new products. This is useful but it is a backward-looking measure. It calibrates the success or failure of previous efforts to launch new products. We also need forward-looking metrics that show how well we are doing in filling the pipeline for future revenues.

Lou Gerstner is the CEO who was brought in to turn around IBM – and he did. He says, 'People don't do what you expect; they do what you inspect.' So if you want innovation, you need to set goals for innovation and measure people in their progress against those goals.

The goals flow from the vision. There is a gap between where we are today and where we want to be. That gap can be expressed as challenges and those challenges can be broken down into goals, objectives and metrics.

Here are some of the types of goals you might set for the year ahead:

- Gain 30 per cent of revenue from products launched in the last two years.

- Launch five new products and make 12 major product enhancements.

- Set up four new strategic partnerships.

- Come up with five new process methods in production and supply.

- Achieve a pipeline of US $40 million of new products in development.

- Have seven ideas per employee implemented from the employee suggestion scheme.

- Gain entry into three new geographic markets.
- Ensure that innovation champions are active and measured in all departments.

A report by the Boston Consulting Group (2006) showed that the three metrics executives consider most valuable are time to market, new product sales and return on investment in innovation. They recommended that in addition other useful metrics are:

- financial resources committed to innovation;
- number of people working on innovation;
- number of ideas generated;
- projected payback from ideas in the pipeline;
- cycle times for the entire process and specific parts;
- number of ideas that move from one stage to the next;
- number of new products or services launched.

There are no perfect measures to choose. You should select the handful of metrics that are most useful for your business. Too few and you are not really tracking the process. But having too many is unwieldy and wasteful. Choose those that align with your corporate goals and then make sure they are monitored at the regular executive review meetings.

7. GET RID OF THE CYNICS

You don't want happy staff – you want passionate staff. You want people who share in the vision and believe that the goals of the organization justify extraordinary efforts. Passion, belief and enthusiasm are great qualities – especially if they are allied with constructive dissent. The ideal companions on your journey want to achieve the same ends as you but they are prepared to challenge your views and to suggest better ways to do things.

However, in most teams there is a mixture ranging from the enthusiastic to the neutral through to the negative and cynical. The leader takes on the task of convincing every one of the benefits of the journey. If, after all your best efforts, there remain one or more people who refuse to buy in, then you have to consider what impact their attitude will have on the rest of the team.

People who are cynical can act like a poison in the body. The negative can undermine the team. Even if they are very competent in their positions it is better to be rid of them. If they cannot be persuaded to support the common purpose, then they should leave in order to pursue something they can believe in.

Many managers find this very difficult. They think that all issues can be resolved by patient discussion. But if all the discussion fails, then you should make the tough decision and move the cynic out. It is better for the cynic and it is better for you.

Mark Goulston, in an article published in *Fast Company* in August 2005, argues that effective leaders move quickly to get rid of the bad apples. Negative situations with difficult people can bring a potentially great company to its knees. He recommends categorizing your people into one of four types – destructive, difficult, good or great. From speaking to top CEOs he advises, 'Recognize and cut the difficult and impossible people early on. Recognize and value good and great people so you can keep them in your life longer.'

8. THROW DOWN A CHALLENGE

A great way to galvanize people into innovative action is to throw down a challenge. Give a specific target and ask for ideas to meet it. Ask a 'how can we… ?' question. How can we halve our customer response time? How can we double our average order value? How can we delight our customers? People respond to challenges and the people closest to the action will often have the best ideas.

When you are facing a difficult issue the temptation is immediately to propose your own ideas or even to force your own solutions. Instead why not ask the group for their best ideas? Give them a deadline. Ask them to come back with a short list of their best proposals and to include a couple of really novel, creative solutions. Then you can discuss them in a constructive way. They may come back with the first idea you had, but now it is their idea and they will take ownership of it. They may return with a terrific idea that would never have crossed your mind. In the unlikely event that they come back with unworkable or unacceptable suggestions, you must not dismiss the ideas out of hand. You must take the time to review them positively and analytically. If you are going to turn down their best ideas, then you need good reasons for doing so. Those reasons must be clear – not political or devious.

A good example of this process is the challenge that President John F Kennedy threw down in 1961. He publicly stated, 'Before this decade is out we will send a man to the moon and return him safely to Earth.' At the time no one knew how it would be done. But the people at NASA enthusiastically took up the challenge and succeeded famously. Ironically, in the decades that followed, when NASA had no clearly articulated challenge, it faltered and lost its momentum.

9. ENCOURAGE DISSENT

The innovative organization has an atmosphere of constructive dissent. Anyone can challenge anything. The more sacred the cow, the more likely it is to be sacrificed. The conventional leaders of years gone by who ruled by command and control are unsuited to a fast-moving entrepreneurial environment. They may be decisive and dynamic but ultimately their reluctance to let go and to allow challenge will limit the motivation of people and the growth of the business.

What you need to encourage is not a lack of respect but a lack of deference. In the modern innovative organization leaders need to earn the respect of their employees because of the values they stand for and not because of their position in the hierarchy. A lack of deference should be encouraged so that anyone can challenge anyone else's ideas regardless of their status.

'Innovation comes from angry and driven people', says Tom Peters. The innovator is not happy with his lot. He is impatient for change. And this can be a problem for successful companies. The natural satisfaction that people derive from success can lead to complacency, which is the enemy of innovation. This is why the innovative leader always engenders a healthy dissatisfaction with the status quo. It is all very well telling shareholders that the company is making steady and satisfactory progress, but the internal message needs more of an edge: 'We are doing well but there is much more to be done. We cannot afford to rest on our laurels.'

Clayton Christensen explains how the very characteristics that make successful companies successful lead them to eschew risky new ventures and keep improving their current products to meet customer demands (Christensen, 2003). In doing so they often miss the next big thing, the new technology that kills them. Polaroid's demise at the hands of digital photography is a salutary example.

In 1901 the radio pioneer Guglielmo Marconi came to England to test his theory that it was possible to send radio signals across the Atlantic. The experts all scoffed at the idea – after all the earth is a giant sphere and radio waves travel in a straight line.

The experts had reason and logic on their side but Marconi was unreasonable and insisted on pursuing his experiment. Amazingly his signal was received. Unknown to the experts (and to Marconi) there is a charged layer around the earth, the ionosphere, which reflected the signal.

Often the innovator has to be obsessive to the point of apparent irrationality in pursuit of his or her dream. The innovator has to be rebellious in opposing conventional wisdom. Anita Roddick, James Dyson, Richard Branson and Stelios were all seen as obstinate angry rebels before they achieved the success that changed their status to visionaries.

So if you want innovators in your team look for people who are passionate about their ideas, who do not defer to authority, who are dissatisfied with the status quo, who are impatient for change and who are angry about the obstacles put in their way. With a profile like that they should certainly stand out from the crowd!

10. BE AN ARSONIST AND A FIRE FIGHTER

Innovative leaders are comfortable with ambiguity. For example, they are arsonists and fire fighters at the same time. They go around starting fires under people – challenging them. They ask questions that confront their teams – the kinds of questions that demand answers and actions:

- Can you find a new route to market?

- Can you halve our service response time?

- How can we break into the Chinese market?

- Can we find a better way to provide this service?

- Can you design a lighter, cheaper, faster version?

The leader starts many initiatives and then follows up to ask how things are going. The projects that are not succeeding are cut back. If the new product prototype does not please customers, or is not technically feasible or is very costly, then lessons are learnt and the team moves on. The leader has a restless curiosity to try new things. Some people may find this frustrating and ask, 'Why does she keep asking us to try new things and then stop them just when they are getting interesting?' The answer is that only by trying lots of different things are we likely to find the radical new initiatives that we need. Not every interesting project can be pursued to completion. Life is too short and resources are limited. It is essential to eliminate the less promising projects so that we can devote resources to those that show the most potential.

Innovative leaders are a little schizophrenic. They applaud success but fear it. They are coldly analytical at some times and hotly passionate at others. Their management styles are sometimes tight and sometimes loose. They start fires and they put them out.

11. THINK LIKE A VENTURE CAPITALIST

The most innovative companies have an approach to trials that is like the philosophy of a venture capitalist (VC). The VC is a prime example of arsonist and fire fighter. He or she will invest in a portfolio of different start-up companies, fully knowing that most will fail. A few might break even and one or two might be successes. But one big success can pay back the costs of all the failures. Despite being smart the VC does not know which ventures will succeed and which will fail, so initially he or she backs them all. As time goes on the VC cuts funding for the failures and gives it to the winners. It is the same with prototypes in business. The leading innovators run many different pilots and measure progress carefully. They chop the losers but pour more resources into the successful trials. That way they are first to market with the real winners.

VCs use a portfolio approach so that they balance the risk of losers with the upsides of winners. They are comfortable with the knowledge that many of the ideas they back will fail.

They are also comfortable with quantity. They receive hundreds or thousands of business proposals every year from all sorts of diverse sources. Many of these have already been rejected by several other VCs, but that doesn't matter. The VC sets his or her own criteria and selects several ideas to support and put into his or her portfolio. If the business plan then misses its targets or milestones, or the customer reaction is poor, or the technology fails to deliver, the VC is sanguine about pulling the plug on this investment. The VC wants to put more resources into the portfolio ideas that are working and is quite relaxed about strangling the losers. If the VC can cut the losses and get out early he or she will.

Contrast this with a typical corporate environment where a small number of new business proposals are considered. A small number are eventually selected and then every effort is made to make them succeed. Failure is abhorred. Extra resources and efforts pour into the CEO's pet project even when the market is screaming that this one won't fly. Emotion and egos come to the fore.

Think like a VC and remember these key points:

- Quantity is good — we want lots of ideas.
- If an idea has been rejected before, we are happy to consider it again.
- We will select the most promising idea using objective criteria.
- We want a return on our innovation portfolio as a whole.
- We know that many of the more radical ideas will probably fail.
- We will focus our resources on the winners and cut resources to the losers.

Why not get a VC to speak at your next executive meeting?

12. BREAK DOWN INTERNAL BARRIERS

Within larger organizations one of the biggest obstacles to innovation is poor internal communication. A 'silo' mentality develops so that departments guard information and ideas rather than share them. People work hard – but in isolated groups. Internal politics can compound the problem, with rivalry and turf wars obstructing collaboration. It can reach the ridiculous stage where the enemy is seen as another department inside the organization rather than the competitors outside.

The leader has to tear down the internal fences, punish internal politics and reward cooperation. This sometimes calls for drastic or innovative actions.

Nokia has an informal rule that no one should eat lunch at their desk or go out for lunch. People are encouraged to eat in the subsidized cafeterias and to mix with diners from outside their department. They have found that the informal meetings across departments are beneficial in sharing ideas and understanding.

Here are some ideas for breaking down internal barriers to communication.

- Publish everyone's objectives and activities on the intranet so that people know what other people are working on.

- Organize cross-functional teams for all sorts of projects. Make them as loose or as formal as you see fit but be sure that there is good mixing and that all the departments involved contribute.

- Arrange plenty of social and extracurricular activities – sports, quizzes, book clubs, hobby clubs, special interest groups, etc.

- Have innovation contests where cross-functional teams compete.

- Deliberately rearrange the office layout from time to time so that people move desks and sit with new groups (or adopt a hot-desk approach).

- Organize a cross-functional innovation incubator (see 'Run an innovation incubator' on page 125).

It is natural for departments in growing organizations to become more insular. As the organization grows, good internal communication becomes more and more difficult. There was a saying in Hewlett Packard – 'If only HP knew what HP knows!' It is the duty of the leader constantly to fight the silting up of internal communications and to force contact and sharing between departments.

13. DESTROY THE HIERARCHY

Some companies have taken the idea of breaking down barriers one step further. They tear up the hierarchical organization and start with something very different.

The traditional top-down structure in organizations can be a powerful inhibitor to innovation. It is a reflection of a style of leadership based on command and control where orders are issued at the top and followed by the ranks. People lower down the organization who have great ideas can feel inhibited about promoting them. They feel it is disrespectful to challenge the command chain. Most modern businesses try to overcome this with open communication and employee empowerment. But there is a more radical alternative – destroy the hierarchy altogether.

Oticon, the innovative Danish hearing-aid manufacturer, broke the conventions of corporate structure when it tore up the hierarchy and created what became known as a 'spaghetti organization'. People are not allocated to departments but move from project to project. The system looks chaotic in a conventional sense but Oticon have achieved remarkable success with it over a period of 10 years.

Another celebrated example of this approach is W L Gore & Associates (UK) Ltd, manufacturer of the world famous GORE-TEX® fabric. In 2006 it was voted number one in *The Sunday Times* '100 Best Companies to Work For' survey – and was the first company to stay top of the list three years in succession.

Gore's unusual approach involves teams forming for projects and selecting their own leaders. There is no formal executive structure and employees are appraised by their peers. On the company's website (accessed in 2006) Associate John Housego, Livingston plant leader, explains: 'You quickly learn what it means to be a real team player. Many companies profess to foster team spirit, but at Gore your contribution is rated not by an individual, but by your immediate team.'

There are many examples on the internet of communities that come together for a common purpose and largely manage themselves. Wikipedia is a good example.

It appears that successful organizations of the future will not resemble the hierarchical structures of the past. They will be fluid, adaptable networks. People will coalesce into teams to accomplish certain tasks and then re-form into new teams. A useful analogy is a theatre company. Here everyone agrees a common goal – a vision of a brilliant team performance. Each person learns their part in the play and fulfils their role in a creative and high-quality manner. Then there is a fresh objective – a new play with a new director. The actors and support staff have entirely different responsibilities. The person who was a star before is now in a supporting role. But everyone shares the common purpose – to put on a great performance and to delight their customers.

14. HAVE YOUR BEST PEOPLE WORKING ON INNOVATION

Many businesses make the mistake of giving innovation projects to junior executives. It seems natural to hand innovation opportunities to enthusiastic and promising upstarts. But generally it is the experienced heavyweights who can overcome all the process and political obstacles that will occur with innovation projects.

In September 1999 Lou Gerstner, CEO of IBM, read a line buried deep in a report which said that current quarter pressures had forced a business unit to cut costs by stopping efforts in a promising new area. Gerstner was incensed and wanted to find out how often this happened. He asked J Bruce Herrald, IBM's senior VP in charge of strategy, to find out. Herrald found a similar pattern in at least 22 other cases. IBM had plenty of new ideas but it had a remarkably hard time turning those ideas into businesses. IBM had produced many crucial inventions, such as the relational database and the router, then watched while others such as Oracle and Cisco built huge companies around these products.

Herrald investigated the causes and found that IBM rewarded short-term results and was reluctant to devote management attention and resources to rolling the dice. IBM's leaders did not spend much time on new businesses and they did not tap their 'A-team' of executives to run them. 'We were relegating this to the most inexperienced people', Herrald is quoted as saying in an article by Alan Deutschman, published in *Fast Company* in March 2005. 'We were not putting the best and brightest talent on this.'

Gerstner and Herrald reversed this approach. They deliberately put their most experienced and talented executives in charge of emerging business opportunities (EBOs). These executives' mission was to find areas new to IBM that could yield profitable billion-dollar-plus businesses in five to seven years. The programme has been a remarkable success. Between 2000 and 2005 IBM launched 25 EBOs. Three failed and were closed down but the remaining 22 produced annual revenues of over US $15 billion and growth of over 40 per cent per year.

More importantly than their revenue impact, the EBOs helped change IBM's culture. 'We've become more willing to experiment, more willing to accept failure, learn from it and move on. Now being an EBO leader is a really desirable job at IBM', says Herrald, in the same article by Alan Deutschman, published in *Fast Company* in March 2005.

The lesson from IBM is clear. If you want to change the culture of an organization so that it values innovation and new business start-ups, then get your most senior and best people involved in these activities. Don't delegate the work to lower-level staff and hope for the best.

15. BE PASSIONATE

People will not follow an unenthusiastic leader. They will follow someone who has a vision and is passionate about it. When we think of Winston Churchill or Martin Luther King or Nelson Mandela we can see that their passion for what they believed in made them great leaders.

Here is an exercise sometimes conducted on leadership courses in pairs – but you can do it on your own. Think for a moment about a key component of your vision for what you want to achieve for the business this year. Choose a single important goal that you as a leader want to accomplish. Now imagine that you expressed that goal to your people in a dull, boring, unenthusiastic way. What would happen? Now consider how you could communicate the goal again, but this time with passion, with energy, with commitment, with enthusiasm. If you were receiving those two kinds of messages how would you react? Which message would inspire you to change your behaviour, to do something extraordinary, to go the extra mile?

The sales training expert Robin Fielder says, 'Never, ever forget that people are more persuaded by your convictions than by your arguments.'

Jim Collins puts it like this: the good to great companies did not say, 'OK folks, let's get passionate about what we do.' Sensibly, they went about it the other way round entirely: 'We should only do those things that we can get passionate about.' Kimberley-Clark executives made the shift to paper-based consumer products in large part because they could get more passionate about them (Collins, 2001: 109).

Focus on the things that you want to change and the most important challenges you face, and be passionate about overcoming them. Your energy and drive will translate itself into direction and inspiration for your people.

It is no good filling your bus with contented, complacent passengers. You want evangelists, passionate supporters; people who believe that reaching the destination is really worthwhile; people who are on a mission to make the world a better place.

This drive and enthusiasm starts with the leader. If you want to inspire people to innovate, to change the way they do things and to achieve extraordinary results, then you have to be passionate about what you believe in and you have to communicate that passion every time you speak.

Section 2:
Problem analysis

1. DIAGNOSE THE CURRENT SITUATION

The vision sets the direction. But before we embark on the journey it is useful to know where we are starting from. An honest and accurate assessment of the competitiveness and innovation capacity of the organization is essential. Most managers are familiar with the SWOT analysis – an appraisal of strengths, weaknesses, opportunities and threats. This should be carried out at both an analytical and emotional level. Hard empirical data from customer surveys, market share data and detailed trend analysis is coupled with informed opinions and feelings about issues such as brand image, technology directions, market trends, fashion and competitors' cultures and intentions.

An innovation audit looks at a number of issues to see what is working well and what is impeding innovation in the company. It asks analytical questions like these:

- How many new products and services did we launch last year and how does this compare to the ideal?

- How long does it take an idea to go from initial approval to full implementation?

- What proportion of our revenues comes from products or services launched in the last two years?

- How effective is our idea generation programme? How many ideas are we generating?

- How healthy is our new product pipeline? What is the forecast value of developments in the pipeline?

- How many ideas per employee are submitted and how many are approved?

- What resources in terms of people, time and money are we allocating to innovation?

In addition to numerical and analytical questions the audit should examine softer issues. In-depth interviews with a sample of people from different departments and levels will reveal much about the culture. Typical discussion points centre around questions like these:

- To what extent are people empowered to try out new ideas?
- Do we recognize and reward risk taking?
- Do we blame people for failure when initiatives do not succeed?
- Can people challenge company policy or the decisions of the boss?
- Are we complacent or entrepreneurial?
- Do we deliberately look outside for ideas?
- Do departments openly collaborate on projects?
- What is stopping us from implementing more ideas quickly?

The audit should also examine the idea approval process. How many hurdles does a proposal have to clear to get approved? How many people are involved? Flow diagrams of the theoretical and real approval processes need to be generated and examined. Is the approval process fit for purpose? Can small ideas get through or do they have to go through the same approvals as major initiatives? And so on.

A good impartial audit will identify key areas for improvement in corporate culture and in innovation processes. It will help you to prioritize the issues that need to be addressed.

2. ANALYSE PROBLEMS

When we are faced with a problem our first instinct is to take action and be seen to be doing something. This is the natural reaction of the macho manager. Sometimes we have to take immediate action. If the building is on fire it is no good calling a meeting to discuss courses of action – the leader needs to be decisive and clear. But if the issue is important though not urgent, then we need a more considered approach. The more complex the problem and the more factors that are involved, the greater the danger that we will jump in at the wrong place.

There are several practical and simple tools that can be used to help analyse problems.   These include Fishbone Analysis, Why, Why? and Lotus Blossom. Why, Why? is covered on page 36. In each of these methods the team identifies as many causes of the problem as it can find and then displays and prioritizes them in a graphical way on a sort of mind map. Another non-graphical approach is Six Serving Men, which is explained on page 38.

The benefits of using a suitable problem analysis tool are considerable:

- It stops you jumping to conclusions.

- It challenges your assumptions about what the real cause of the problem is.

- It helps give everyone in the team a common understanding of the underlying issues.

- It helps prioritize where you should put your efforts.

- It can give you a sequence of items to tackle – a road map for solving the problem.

- It helps you to see connections between underlying causes.

- Different people or different teams will come up with different analyses, which give you fresh insights into the possible causes of the problem.

3. ASK 'WHY, WHY?'

Small children often use a method of questioning that consists of a stream of questions – each starting with 'Why?' Each time you give the child an answer they ask 'Why?' again. This problem analysis method is based on that principle. The problem is stated and then the question 'Why?' is asked. It may be asked in the form of 'Why did this happen?' or 'Why is this a problem?' That question should elicit some initial main answers. For each of these answers the question 'Why?' is then asked again. This process is repeated until a full picture of all the causes is shown.

If, for example, the problem was poor results from brainstorming meetings, the initial Why? diagram might look like the one on page 37.

The process can be extended to more levels – here for instance by asking why is there no confidence in the process or why is there a risk-averse culture.

The Why, Why? method is a simple but powerful way of showing all the probable causes of an issue. It is fine for complex problems – though you will need a large wall as you go down several levels with the questions.

It is good to get several small groups each to do their own Why, Why? analysis and then to compare results. This can often reveal unexpected insights.

As with all problem analysis techniques the purpose is not to solve the problem but to understand the underlying causes before attempting to find solutions. It helps people to see the overall nature of the problem and the interrelated causes. It can help you to prioritize which areas to focus on first and it can give you a prototype project plan for solving the problem.

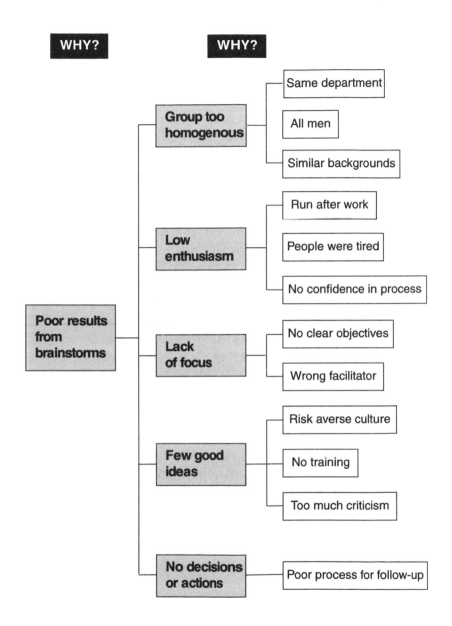

Figure 1 A Why Why diagram

4. USE SIX SERVING MEN

Six Serving Men is an excellent questioning technique. It provides a simple, disciplined approach for probing a situation from 12 different points of view.

It is based on the poem by Rudyard Kipling:

I keep six honest serving men, they taught me all I knew,

Their names are What and Why and When and How and Where and Who.

We probe the topic using these questioning words from both a positive and a negative perspective. The issue is defined and then 12 sheets of flipchart paper are arranged around the room. On each sheet one of the 12 questions is written as the heading and the team then comes up with answers to that question. Suppose the issue is 'We need to improve innovation.' The questions could be constructed as follows:

- What is innovation for us?

- What is not innovation?

- Why do we sometimes get innovation?

- Why do we not get innovation?

- When do we get innovation? (Or when are our people innovative?)

- When do we not get innovation?

- How do we get innovation?

- How do we impede innovation?

- Where in our organization do we get innovation?

- Where do we get no innovation?

- Who is innovative?

- Who is not innovative? (Or who is blocking innovation?)

We ask each question in a very literal way. So the 'when' questions refer to times of day, days of the week, months of the year as well as a more generic 'when'. By repeatedly asking these questions we force ourselves to approach the problem from different angles. In addition to routine answers the method will typically unearth some unusual perspectives and insights. A different light is shone upon the problem. The ideas that come out give us a variety of options for tackling the problem. We prioritize these and move forward into idea generation.

5. REDEFINE THE PROBLEM

One simple technique that can generate fresh thinking is to redefine the problem. The way we express any issue, the form and choice of words we use, sets expectations and constraints. There was an ideas meeting at a manufacturing plant where shop floor workers were asked for their suggestions on how to improve productivity. The response was disappointingly sparse. A little later a similar group was asked to brainstorm the challenge 'How can we make your job easier?' The result was a flood of good ideas. Most of the ideas that came out were fundamentally productivity improvement ideas. Just by changing the question and giving it a different focus results were transformed.

If you have laboured with an issue for a while, stop and ask the group to redefine the problem using none of the original words. Say, for example, we are an insurance company and the initial challenge is 'How can we improve company brand awareness?' Now everyone, working silently, has to express the same aim in different words. The emphasis is not on finding slavish synonyms but on expressing the essential goal or meaning in a new way. So people might suggest the following:

- Get more people to know us.
- Make customers think of us first.
- Get drivers to think of us before they have an accident.
- Double the number of people who telephone us.
- Be the first choice for insurance companies.
- Be the first recommendation of brokers.
- When people think insurance they think of our name first.
- Be in front of people.
- Make our name the best known of local businesses.

In this process there is no 'right answer'. Each re-forming of the issue gives a different perspective. We could now select some of the most promising and brainstorm them. For instance, one group might consider, 'How can we get customers to think of us first?' Another group might use as the starting point, 'How can we be the first recommendation of brokers?' Because each group has a slightly different focus for its idea generation they are likely to come up with different ideas.

6. ASK 'WHAT BUSINESS ARE WE IN?'

The CEO of Black and Decker once said, 'People don't go into a DIY store because they need one of our drills. They go because they need a hole in the wall.' Wonderbra, in their internal communications to staff say, 'We do not sell underwear. We do not sell lingerie. What we sell is self-confidence for women.' Harley Davidson does not sell motorbikes. It sells the concept of freedom to middle-aged men.

Conversely many companies that did do not know what business they were in went out of business. For example:

- Companies that thought they were in the horse-drawn carriage business but were really in transportation were wiped out by automobiles.

- Companies that thought they were in the ice supply business but were really in food and drink storage were eliminated by refrigerators.

- Companies that made slide rules and failed to realize they were in the technical calculation business were made obsolete by graphics calculators.

- Companies that thought they were in the CD business but were really in music were replaced by digital downloads.

- Companies that thought they were in the typewriter business but were really in communications were put out of business by the word processor.

What business are you in? Why do your customers buy the goods or services you provide? There are several ways to find out:

- Ask your customers.

- Ask people who consider your product but do not buy it.

- Observe your customers and how they use your product.

And of course the answer may well be different for different customers. Some people choose a certain make of car to make them look good, others to feel safe and others to enjoy the ride. Unless you know exactly why prospective customers will buy your product you are unable to properly market or sell. Worse still, you will be blind to the alternatives, the opportunities and the threats that exist.

Do not define your business by your product but by the benefit you deliver to your customer. (See the box above for examples of how not to do this.) So instead of saying, 'We make typewriters', say, 'We help people communicate effectively.' Instead of saying, 'We are an innovation management consultancy', say, 'We help clients develop new sources of revenue and profit.'

One definition of innovation in business is an action that extends customer value. So if we want to innovate we need to understand what it is that the customer really values. Then we can set our minds to the task of how to extend that value. Start every week by asking these two questions:

What do customers really value?

What business are we in?

Section 3:
Generating ideas

1. HAVE A SUGGESTIONS SCHEME

Every organization that has more than a handful of employees should have a suggestions scheme. It is one of the best ways of benefiting from the creative ideas of your people. Unfortunately suggestions schemes sometimes have a bad image. People associate them with a box on the wall where a few ideas are put in and then nothing much happens. Modern staff suggestions schemes are focused on the right goals. They are fast and responsive. They use specialist software and intranet sites that are easy to use.

Siemens Automation and Drives is a good example. They employ 400 people in Congleton, Cheshire making electric motor drives. Their scheme is called Ideas Unlimited. It generates over 4,000 suggestions a year, of which about 75 per cent are implemented. The total annual savings run to some £770,000 (US $1.44 million).

Howard Ball, who administers the scheme part-time, says that the key is simplicity. There are no forms and no paperwork. The intranet application has just four screens – entering the idea, evaluating, accepting or rejecting, and implementing. Every manager acts as an evaluator. Payments are made in the form of vouchers – maximum £50 (US $90) – on acceptance of the idea. Howard Ball is convinced that small rewards and recognition on acceptance are a better incentive than larger rewards delayed until implementation.

Another interesting aspect of the Siemens scheme is that the company publishes league tables of ideas implemented by departments, with awards for the most successful departments. Managers are incentivized to accept and implement ideas.

Emma Akerman at Siemens suggested that a component be made out of galvanized steel instead of stainless steel. The idea was accepted and will save around £60,000 a year. She says, 'The fact that you can put in suggestions online makes it easier, and knowing you can contribute ideas means you take more interest in your work.'

The main problem that had to be overcome according to Howard Ball was getting factory workers to use computers.

They were not regular PC users, so a training and help programme was put in place. Another thing to watch out for is evaluator overload – you have to give time and recognition to those who assess the suggestions. But, overall, Ideas Unlimited is a big success. The company started with a target of six implemented ideas per employee and achieved more than seven. The next year's target was nine. Howard's final piece of advice is this, 'Keep benchmarking, keep involving and keep consulting.'

Toyota gets around 2 million ideas a year in its employee suggestions scheme. Most of the ideas are approved and implemented.

At Best Buy all 128,000 employees are encouraged to contribute ideas. Nate Omann, a project manager in services, noticed that many flat-panel TVs were damaged during delivery. He suggested a 'TV taco', a reusable device that looks like a large taco. It goes around the TV to protect it. 'This idea is going to save us millions of dollars', says Sari Ballard, Executive VP of Human Resources at Best Buy, reported in *Fast Company* in November 2006. 'And from a customer perspective, which matters even more, we get it right the first time we deliver.'

Great suggestion schemes are focused, easy to use, well resourced, responsive and open to all. They do not need to offer huge rewards. Recognition and response are generally more important. Above all they have to have the wholehearted commitment of the senior team to keep them fresh, properly managed and successful.

2. RUN IDEAS EVENTS

If there is an important issue that needs some creative ideas, then why not set a specific challenge for it and run some ideas events? Declare the challenge in specific terms and the criteria that will be used to select the best idea and then let the proceedings begin. Here are the sorts of events you could run:

- A lunchtime brainstorm with pizza and drinks.

- A team contest where teams post ideas on an intranet site and everyone can vote for their favourite.

- A game based on a reality TV show where people vote out the worst ideas and the number of contestants is whittled down to a winner.

- A party where people have to contribute ideas to get treats such as snacks and drinks.

- An ideas event where you bring in some external people to ensure diverse thinking. They could be suppliers, customers, students or relatives of employees.

By running an event you focus attention and energy on the issue. People know that it is important and therefore they will make an effort. The event registers in their subconscious minds and the result should be a wealth of ideas. In addition the event will often be motivational, team building and fun.

Set a deadline for submission of ideas. That will help concentrate people's minds. Also, show ideas that have already been submitted so as to avoid duplication. This also allows contributors to build on other people's ideas.

3. ALLOW LINE MANAGER BYPASS

Whatever suggestion scheme or idea initiation events you implement, it is important to ensure that there is a facility for individuals to bypass their line manager if necessary.

Line managers can be resistant to ideas from their own people for a variety of reasons. They might fear that the person making the suggestion might be taken away from them to implement it. They might think that the idea does not reflect well on their department. They might see some implicit criticism of themselves in the suggestion. They might have political agendas or prejudices that lead them to block ideas coming from their team. If all ideas require initial sign-off by the first line manager, then the flow of ideas will be inhibited in some areas.

When Lou Gerstner first took over the reins as CEO of IBM one of his first actions was to allow anyone, anywhere in the company to e-mail him with ideas and suggestions. He received a flood of input — much of which gave him useful information on what the real problems were at the grass roots. Sir Richard Branson has long had a policy that employees can bypass formal idea submission procedures and come straight to him with a business proposal if they are convinced that is the best route.

Allowing people to bypass the normal chain of command provides an essential safety valve that enables radical ideas to be viewed dispassionately at some distance from their source.

4. PLAN YOUR BRAINSTORM MEETINGS

Everyone has participated in a brainstorm meeting to generate ideas at some stage. But many managers stop using them after some indifferent experiences. Brainstorms, however, remain one of the simplest and best ways to generate good ideas quickly.

There are some key things to bear in mind before running a brainstorm – little things can make the difference between success and failure. So try giving your answers to the list of brainstorm meetings questions below.

How many people should there be in a brainstorm meeting?

- What sort of people should you invite?
- How long should the brainstorm meeting be?
- Who should facilitate the meeting?
- How will you capture the ideas?
- What criteria should you use to evaluate ideas?

Let's take a look at the issues.

HOW MANY PEOPLE SHOULD THERE BE IN A BRAINSTORM MEETING?

Between 6 and 10 is ideal. If you have fewer than 6 there may be not enough divergent sources of ideas. If you have more than 10 or 11 the mechanics don't work so well and not everyone can be heard or get their ideas recorded. So if you have 16 people, for example, it is better to divide into two groups of 8 and have parallel brainstorms.

WHAT SORT OF PEOPLE SHOULD YOU INVITE?

The key point here is diversity. If you have the same group of people who have been struggling with an issue for months and you put them into a brainstorm meeting then the chances are that you will get many of the same old ideas again. However, if you sprinkle in some outsiders, then you are more likely to generate fresh suggestions.

You want a mixture of people to contribute – young and old, male and female, experienced and fresh into the company, inside and outside the department, etc. Sometimes it is good to ask a client or a supplier to join you if the issue is appropriate. Be sure to ask someone who is lively and likely to come up with some provocative questions and ideas.

HOW LONG SHOULD THE BRAINSTORM MEETING BE?

It depends how complex the issue is, how many methods you plan to use and whether you need to do some problem analysis work first. For a regular brainstorm meeting where the problem is reasonably well defined, an hour is plenty. In any event it is better to have a short, high-energy meeting than a long rambling one.

People are generally brighter and fresher in the morning. So why not start at 8.30 am with coffee and muffins before they can get distracted with e-mails, telephone calls and today's crises?

WHO SHOULD FACILITATE THE MEETING?

The best answer is to have a skilled external facilitator. This is someone experienced, neutral, enthusiastic – and with good handwriting. They manage the flow of ideas by encouraging everyone to contribute. They intervene if some people become too dominant or take the meeting in wrong directions. They can use a variety of methods to keep ideas flowing. If you cannot get an external facilitator, choose someone enthusiastic and neutral on the issues. If their writing is not so good, then delegate someone else as the chart writer (sometimes called the scribe). This is not necessarily the department manager! Generally speaking the department manager carries a lot of baggage and their presence as scribe or meeting leader can inhibit people from voicing controversial or disruptive ideas.

HOW WILL YOU CAPTURE THE IDEAS?

The three most popular ways to record ideas are on flipcharts, on reusable sticky notes and on computer. Flipcharts are quick and easy. Everyone can see the ideas as they are written up. Sticky notes are a little messy in the idea generation stage but their flexibility comes into its own in the evaluation stage when they can be moved around or grouped very easily. There are also software programmes that allow you to capture, display and sort your ideas quickly and easily.

WHAT CRITERIA SHOULD YOU USE TO EVALUATE IDEAS?

Many brainstorm meetings start without any agreed criteria for how the best proposals will be chosen. A selection method is needed but it is easy to set criteria that are too restrictive – eg 'We want ideas that can be implemented this quarter with no additional resource.' A good test is whether you are a FAN of the idea – ie is it Feasible, Attractive and Novel? See more on idea evaluation on page 57.

The brainstorm meeting should have a clear objective. This should be expressed as a desired outcome rather than a preferred approach. So 'How can we improve sales?' is good but a little too vague. 'How can we increase our prospect conversion rate?' is good but a little too prescriptive. 'How can we increase sales by 50 per cent?' is better. It sets a clear and challenging goal but is quite unconstrained as to how to get there.

5. BRAINSTORM MEETINGS – GENERATE GREAT IDEAS

If you are facilitating a brainstorm meeting, there are a number of basic things you can do to make the meeting work effectively. The first is to recognize the three phases of the meeting:

- The meeting starts with a definition of the problem or objective.

- The idea generation phase uses divergent, creative thinking to generate a large number of ideas.

- The idea evaluation phase uses convergent and analytical thinking to select the best ideas to carry forward.

During the idea generation phase it is important that the participants understand and abide by the rules, so spell them out:

- Suspend judgement — no criticism of ideas is allowed during this phase. All ideas are welcomed, no matter how bizarre or silly.

- All ideas are recorded and numbered. The ideas are written down (or keyed into a computer) as short, specific action-oriented statements.

- Participants piggy-back on each other's ideas so each idea can trigger further ideas.

- Quantity is good. We want a great many ideas.

You can record the ideas using flipcharts, reusable sticky notes or direct onto a computer programme. The facilitator and chart writer (or scribe) is usually the same person, but you can split the roles. The facilitator keeps the energy level high and encourages the flow of ideas without favouring particular individuals or ideas.

If there is a pause in the flow of ideas don't worry. People may just be thinking. You can always use the techniques outlined in 'Juice up your brainstorm meetings' on page 59.

Often the first ideas are the most obvious, routine suggestions. The later ideas are more bizarre and creative. So keep going until you have reached an impressive total – 80 to 100 ideas is not uncommon.

6. BRAINSTORM MEETINGS – EVALUATE THE IDEAS

The evaluation phase of the process is critical to the success of the session and typically needs as much time and attention as the idea generation stage. In evaluation we switch from suspending judgement to exercising critical judgement in order to whittle down the ideas to a shortlist of actionable items. Try to agree the selection criteria in advance so that you have a basis for selecting the strongest proposals.

Say you are analysing ideas for new products. The criteria you agree might well be:

- Will customers like it?
- Is it technically feasible?
- Will it make money?

Each idea is then assessed against these measures. It is better to have a short list of broad conceptual criteria than a long list of detailed rules. Many managers like to include the question 'Can it be done soon and with current resources?' However, these kinds of restrictive criteria often mean that good radical ideas get discarded.

A recommended general set of criteria for all sorts of ideas is the FAN method, as previously described. Are you a FAN of the idea? Is it feasible – can we make it? Does the technology exist? Is it attractive – does it appeal to us and to customers? Is it novel – is it something new for our organization?

If you have a long list of ideas to evaluate, then the usual method is for the facilitator to go through each item and canvass opinions. Ideas are ranked as excellent (with two ticks), interesting (with one tick) or they are crossed out. This can be a long-winded process, so here are some quicker methods:

- Each person comes to the front and puts ticks next to their favourite ideas. The ideas with the most ticks go forward. This method is quick and energetic but it does mean that some of the more obscure ideas may be overlooked.

- There is a secret ballot and people write on slips of paper their favourite ideas. This overcomes the problem of political correctness where people may be afraid to support controversial ideas or may be influenced by the more powerful voices in the room. There is no discussion during the ballot but once the ideas are ranked the group discussion can begin.

- Each person in turn states their favourite idea. The facilitator goes around the room and gives everyone the opportunity to speak. This is quick and interactive but it means that the people who speak later can be unduly influenced by what has gone before.

Once you have selected the best ideas you should assign actions for follow up. Ask people to estimate the resources needed and the next steps. Implement the quick wins immediately and start the planning process for the more complex ideas.

> The UK's largest and most successful supermarket chain, Tesco, uses the following criteria to evaluate ideas; is the idea 'better, simpler and cheaper'? Each of these criteria is put into context. Is the idea better for customers? Is it simpler for staff? Is it cheaper for Tesco? Ideally, new proposals should satisfy all three tests. All staff are encouraged to submit suggestions and they are given a fast response when they do so. Using these clear criteria has helped focus submissions and speed up evaluation.

7. JUICE UP YOUR BRAINSTORM MEETINGS

If your brainstorm meeting runs out of ideas and energy, then it is time to turn to some advanced techniques to boost performance. Here are three of the most effective. There are more in the e-book *How to Generate Ideas* (Sloane, P).

REVERSE THE PROBLEM

Brainstorm the exact opposite of the challenge. If, for example, the question is 'How can we improve customer service?', it is restated as 'How can we make customer service worse?' People will readily think of ideas to drive customers away. Once you have 12 to 20 of these ideas take them in turn. For each one, see what positive ideas to improve customer service can be generated by reversing the idea. For example, 'Don't answer the phone' might lead to 'Answer the phone in two rings' or 'Answer the phone using the customer's name'.

RANDOM WORD

Pick up a dictionary and choose a noun at random. Write the word on the top of the flipchart paper and then underneath list five or six attributes of that word. Then force connections between the word or its attributes and the problem to be solved. You will find that all sorts of new associations spring to mind.

SIMILES

You state the challenge and then get everyone to write down on their own sheet of paper 'Our problem is like...' and then complete the sentence. They must do this in silence so that they are not influenced by each other's ideas. The likenesses do not have to be accurate – they are feelings rather than exact analogies, but each can act as a trigger. You then write out everyone's simile and the group chooses the one that they think is the best analogy for the initial challenge. You brainstorm the chosen simile to find solutions for that problem. You then analyse the ideas to see if any will translate to the original problem and give a working solution there.

So if the challenge was how to motivate the team, you might end up brainstorming how to get children to do their homework. Or instead of how to beat Microsoft, you might brainstorm how a small baker's shop could compete against a supermarket. Each idea in the simile is then considered to see if it can be translated back to your original setting.

8. BRING IN UNRELATED EXPERTS

If you are planning a creative thinking session around a particular topic one way to help displace your thinking and inspire ideas is to bring in experts in the field but from entirely unrelated businesses.

A company had an issue with its sales force. Morale was low and team spirit was poor. Sales people complained about poor leads and poor commissions but the company directors were sure the real problems lay with the motivation and drive of the sales team. So they planned a creative thinking session and put together a team to tackle this problem. They started the meeting with a talk from an outside expert – a major who had served many years in the Army and knew how the Armed Services recruited, trained and motivated its staff. How did the organization instil courage, team spirit, discipline and drive? It certainly was not through bonuses and commissions. The major gave a presentation and the team members asked him questions. Later in the meeting they were able to adapt many of the major's ideas into workable improvements of their own. They improved leadership, training and recognition (even giving a form of medal for the most sales calls in a month) and transformed the performance of the team.

If you are concerned about human resource issues consider getting a completely different point of view by bringing in an external speaker, such as:

- a bishop;
- the head teacher of a school;
- a hospital manager;
- the director of a charity;
- a zoo keeper;
- an army officer;
- the manager of a large hotel.

If you want to improve creativity, design or innovation you might start your meeting with a talk from:

- a film director;
- an interior designer;
- a website designer;
- an advertising agency creative director;
- a chef.

Leaders in other walks of life have faced similar problems to yours but in very different circumstances. See if you can find people to share their experiences with you. Their different views on life can be enlightening and will help displace you from your comfort zone and kick start your creativity.

9. USE A FACILITATOR

If you have an important meeting at which creative or strategic issues are to be discussed, think about using a facilitator. This is particularly true if it is a large group or if there are forceful personalities involved. Many important meetings fail because they fall foul of these types of problems:

- People are inhibited from voicing their opinions; they feel that they will annoy someone important or that they will suffer ridicule or humiliation.

- The loudest voices dominate the discussion.

- Two people get into an argument and neither will give way.

- Too much time is consumed in the early part of the meeting and the agenda is squeezed. The meeting does not run to time.

- No one summarizes agreed action points, so it is unclear what was agreed and what will happen next.

- The most senior person present uses the meeting to push through his or her ideas. People feel railroaded and ignored.

Using a skilled external facilitator overcomes these problems. Facilitators are neutral as regards the content and concerned only with making the process work. Since they have no vested position on any of the issues, they cannot consider any point of view wrong or unacceptable. They welcome all input. They will ensure that the meeting runs to time and will focus on achieving the outcomes that you have set. They will use appropriate methods to encourage discussion. They will draw out quiet people. Equally importantly, they will professionally manage those who are noisy or difficult. They will keep you to time and to the topics in hand.

A good facilitator is particularly useful in a brainstorming or creative thinking meeting. The facilitator can use novel and interesting methods to break the ice, to analyse issues, to generate ideas, to evaluate ideas and to summarize actions. Delegates are much more likely to engage in new activities and to be uninhibited when a complete outsider is the organizer rather than their boss.

10. BREAK THE RULES

How often do you hear leaders using sport as an analogy for their business? We need teamwork like Real Madrid. We want performance like the Ferrari Formula One team. We want commitment like the Europeans in the Ryder Cup. Sport has great attributes in terms of endeavour, teamwork and training but it is a very poor metaphor for business in one important respect — innovation. This is because in sport there are strict rules that cannot be broken without penalty, whereas in business most of the rules can be broken. Radical innovation means contradicting convention and inventing an entirely new game.

If you can find a way to rewrite the rules of the game so that it suits you rather than your competitors, then you can gain a remarkable advantage. In the late 1970s the Swiss watch industry was suffering from fierce competition from the Japanese. Major brands like Omega, Longines and Tissot were in serious trouble. Nicholas Hayek took dramatic action. He merged two of the largest Swiss watch manufacturers ASUAG and SSIH to form a new company, Swatch. It took a radically different approach to watch design, creating a low-cost, high-tech, artistic watch that people reacted to emotionally. Within five years the new company was the largest watch maker in the world. Swatch rewrote the rules of the watch industry. Swiss watches had competed against mass-produced brands by focusing on tradition and quality, but Swatch changed the parameters by making watches that were fun, fashionable and collectable.

Every business operates in an environment of written and unwritten rules. Many of these boundaries and restrictions are self-imposed and accepted without questioning. Often it is the newcomer to an industry who can ask the question, 'What would happen if we broke the rules?'

Richard Branson broke the rules when he launched Virgin Atlantic to take on the major airlines such as British Airways, American Airlines and Pan Am. They all followed the same rules; first class passengers enjoyed the best service, business passengers received adequate service and economy passengers got very few frills. Branson eliminated first class and instead gave first-class service to business passengers. He introduced innovations such as free drinks for economy passengers, videos in headrests and limousine service to the airport.

Anita Roddick, founder of the retail chain the Body Shop, succeeded by deliberately doing the opposite of what the industry experts did. She saw that most pharmacies were stuffy places that sold toiletries, perfumes and medicinal creams in expensive packaging and pretty bottles. She did the opposite by packaging the goods in Body Shop stores in cheap, plastic bottles with plain labels. It saved cost and it made a statement that the contents of the packages were what mattered. The Body Shop was seen as natural, spiritual and in tune with an environmentally friendly consumer.

Picasso broke the rules on what a face should look like and Gaudi broke the rules on what a building should look like. To achieve radical innovation you have to challenge all the assumptions that govern how things should look in your environment. Business is not like sport with well-defined rules and referees. It is more like art. It is rife with opportunity for the lateral thinker who can create new ways to provide the goods and services that customers want.

11. DEFINE YOUR IDEAL COMPETITOR

Take your group and divide them into teams of four to six people. The brief is simple. Imagine that an immensely wealthy corporation has decided to enter your business market. This corporation plans to create a powerful competitor that will use innovative approaches to seize your current organization's customers and wipe you out. It will deliberately exploit your weaknesses to hurt you in the marketplace. This corporation has hired your team to put together the new competitor and given you immense resources. What would you do?

Each team has to brainstorm innovative ways of reaching the customer, delivering better services and seizing a leading market share. They start with a clean slate; with none of the legacies, encumbrances or excuses that are holding you back. They can adopt any technology they want and have virtually unlimited resources. Once the constraints are off it is much easier to conceive of radical, innovative business models.

To take this process to the next stage ask each team to choose a model and then to answer three questions. What does the model look like? What kind of organization would be best placed to exploit this and, finally, what should we be doing about this?

The teams present back their ideas and the moderator decides on a winner. The emphasis is placed on creative ideas rather than undercutting on price or out-spending on promotions. Obviously, many of the ideas generated are ones that your organization should be investigating urgently before a real 'ideal competitor' emerges.

12. TRY WEIRD COMBINATIONS

A weird combination that worked for the BBC is their celebrity stock exchange, Celebdaq (www.bbc.co.uk/celebdaq). On this site you can take a future option on the media coverage for your chosen celebrity and then watch your option rise or fall in value. By marrying *Hello!* magazine and financial spread betting the BBC has created a radical innovation that is proving very popular.

Marrying ideas has been around a long time. What is the greatest invention of all? One contender is Johannes Gutenberg's printing press. Before Gutenberg, all books had been laboriously copied out by hand or stamped out with wood blocks. Around 1450 in Strasbourg, Gutenberg combined two ideas to invent a method of printing with moveable type. He coupled the flexibility of a coin punch with the power of a wine press. His invention enabled the production of books and the spread of knowledge and ideas throughout the Western World. In terms of revolutionizing communication only the invention of the internet comes close.

When you combine two ideas to make a third, two plus two can equal five. In the ancient world one of the great discoveries was that by combining two soft metals – copper and tin – you could create a strong alloy – bronze. In a similar way, combining two minor inventions – the coin punch and the wine press — gave birth to the mighty printing press.

Try combining your main product or service with a range of foreign concepts and see what you get. By putting together toys and management training Lego was able to conceive a new corporate strategy technique whereby management teams build business models using Lego blocks. By combining the worlds of pharmaceuticals and fashion, L'Oreal has carved out a distinctive and successful strategy.

How can a concert violinist create an innovation? The acclaimed Finnish violinist Linda Brava has performed with many leading symphony orchestras. She was elected to Helsinki city council in 1996 and became Finnish Tourism ambassador to Sweden. She posed for *Playboy* magazine and appeared on the

US TV series *Baywatch*. By combining glamour with virtuosity in classical music she has established a unique brand for herself.

Take a product and think of an absurd way to make it work. Trevor Bayliss is the English inventor who conceived the clockwork radio. What a strange combination! Radios need electricity and clockwork is a mechanical method. Surely batteries or mains electricity are better ways to power a radio. However, in the developing world batteries are expensive and mains electricity is unreliable. Bayliss built a reliable radio that people could wind up by hand. It has transformed the availability of information in many of the poorest regions of the Earth.

You can apply the same process to combinations of partners and think of diverse individuals or organizations who could work with you. Combining your different skills could create an original approach to the market. Think of how Pavarotti performed with the Irish rock band U2. Or how Mercedes-Benz and Swatch combined to create the revolutionary Smart Car. Who would have thought that a prestige carmaker would collaborate with a fashion watchmaker to come up with the most innovative town car ever seen?

Nearly every new idea is a synthesis of other ideas. So a great way to generate ideas is to force combinational possibilities. Get your team together and brainstorm how you could mix your products with those from wildly different sources. Take it to the extreme. How could you combine your key concept with random products, services, places, personalities, etc? The more bizarre the combination, the more original the ideas that are triggered.

David Musselwhite wanted to break down the inhibitions that stopped people having initial discussions with his law firm. So, with his wife, he set up Legal Grounds, a combination of a law firm and a coffee shop. Prospective clients could order a coffee and have an informal consultation with a lawyer. The publicity coverage has been enormous and significant new business has resulted (Woolf, 2001: 108).

Study how your customers use your products or services. Do they use them with other products? Is there a combination you could create that would make things easier for your customers?

One example is the drinks company that innovated with a ready-mixed gin and tonic.

Remember that:

- Someone put a trolley and a suitcase together and got a suitcase with wheels.

- Someone put an igloo with a hotel and got an ice palace.

- Someone put a copier and a telephone together and got a fax machine.

- Someone put a bell and a clock together and got an alarm clock.

- Someone put a coin punch and a wine press together and we got books.

So the next time you wheel your suitcase or read a fax or a book you are benefiting from someone's ingenuity in putting together a combination of ideas. Why not try it with your own products to drive innovation in your business?

13. GO FOR QUANTITY

One of the problems with the Western education system is that it teaches that for most questions there is one correct answer. Examinations with multiple choice questions force the student to try to select the right answer and avoid the wrong ones. So when our young people leave school they are steeped in a system that says find the 'right answer' and you have solved the problem. Unfortunately the real world is not like that. For almost every problem there are multiple solutions. We have to unlearn the school approach and instead adopt an attitude of always looking for more and better answers.

To be really creative you need to generate a large number of ideas before you refine the process down to a few to test out. To make your organization more innovative you have to increase the yield. Why do you need more ideas? Because when you start generating ideas you generate the obvious, easy answers. As you come up with more and more ideas, so you produce more wacky, crazy, creative ideas – the kind that can lead to really radical solutions.

The management guru Gary Hamel talks about 'corporate sperm count' – the virility test of how many ideas your business generates. Many managers fear that too many ideas will be unmanageable but the most innovative companies revel in multitudes of ideas.

When BMW launched its Virtual Innovation Agency (VIA) to canvass suggestions from people all round the world it received 4,000 ideas in the first week. And the ideas continue to roll in. If you go to www.bmw.com and click on innovation you can make your own contribution to BMW's idea bank.

The Toyota Corporation in-house suggestion scheme generates some 2 million ideas a year. Even more remarkably, over 90 per cent of the suggestions are implemented. Quantity works.

Thomas Edison was prolific in his experiments. His development of the electric light took over 9,000 experiments and that of the storage cell around 50,000. He still holds the record for the most patents – over 1,090 in his name. After his death 3,500 notebooks full of his ideas and jottings were found. It was the prodigiousness of his output that led to so many breakthroughs. Picasso painted over 20,000 works. Bach composed at least one work a week. The great geniuses produced quantity as well as quality. Sometimes it is only by producing the many that we can produce the great.

When you start brainstorming or using other creative techniques the best idea might not come in the first 20 or the first 100 ideas. The quality of ideas does not degrade with quantity – often the later ideas are the more radical ones from which a truly lateral solution can be developed.

What do you do when you have a mountain of ideas and suggestions? You sort them, analyse them and try out those with the most potential. You set criteria against which you can evaluate the ideas. (See 'Brainstorm meetings – evaluate the ideas' on page 57). The really promising ideas are critically examined from the perspectives of technical feasibility, customer acceptance and profitability. If they pass these hurdles they move rapidly to a prototype phase. They are then tested in the harsh reality of the marketplace where a sort of accelerated Darwinism occurs – only the fittest survive. The interesting ideas should be kept in a database and allowed to incubate. When you revisit them later you may well find that you now see a way to adapt or combine them into something worthwhile.

14. TRY A DIFFERENT ENVIRONMENT

A great way to juice up your creativity sessions is to choose a different environment. A conference room inside your regular office building is easy and convenient – but it is also familiar, dull and lacking in stimulation. People are tempted to wander off back to their desks at breaks, to read their e-mails or to chat to colleagues.

The normal alternative to the office is an off-site meeting at a local hotel. But this is not much better. Hotel meeting rooms are typically bland, anodyne and boring. By choosing somewhere more radical you send a message that delegates will be out of the office and can think 'out of the office' thoughts.

Here are some venues that have been successfully used for creative thinking meetings:

- A zoo. Delegates walk around the zoo and choose an animal. On their return they have to argue passionately why their animal should be used as a model for the company. They focus on the animal's attributes – for example, an owl has great vision and what we need is to establish a clear vision to replace conflicting messages.

- An art gallery or a museum. A business challenge is issued and then the delegates wander around the place drawing inspiration and stimulation from the paintings or artefacts they see. They return bursting with ideas.

- A football (or other sports) stadium. Delegates can walk on the pitch and see the sports photos and memorabilia. Sports metaphors abound.

- A castle or stately home. What lessons from history can we learn and apply today? What would the great entrepreneurs, leaders, innovators and empire-builders of the past have done with our types of challenge?

John R. Hoke III is Nike Inc.'s chief design guru. One way that he sets conditions to arouse his team is with 'design inspiration trips'. He sends his team to the zoo to observe and sketch animals' feet. He'll hold a lecture on the glass sculptures of Dale Chihuly or bring in Eva Zeisel to discuss structure and forms. The Detroit car show is an annual pilgrimage that he makes and his reason for going is more about drawing inspiration from sleek lines, styling and colour schemes than fascination with automobiles. 'I go to the show, and I'm not even looking at cars', Hoke says. 'I'm looking at form, surfacing, and silhouette. I'm looking at the assembly of materials, the depth of colour.' One design camp involved an excursion into origami with its rigorous focus on constraints. Designers were asked to build an ergonomic chair out of cardboard. Instead of conventional glues, participants had to concentrate on folding and bending. Then Hoke threw in another twist: The judging would be based on whether the new seats could hold people in a contest of musical chairs. Hoke also brought in an Israeli origami artist as a tutor, and 'we had designers fold paper for three days', he says. 'The ideas that have come from that session are phenomenal. It forced us to look deeper at flexibility and how geometry works.' Instead of cutting and sewing, he says, 'what about crimping, folding, and bending?' (Hoke, quoted from an article in *Business Week* published on 28 November 2005).

A change of environment can help engender a change in attitudes, so think about changing the environment in your office and also about using entirely different venues. Being somewhere novel will assist your people to think novel thoughts.

15. CONCEIVE A DIFFERENT BUSINESS MODEL

Is there a completely different way to operate in your business? If all your competitors are using a broadly similar approach, is there an entirely separate approach that could deliver what your customers want?

In the early 1980s the leading manufacturers of PCs were companies such as IBM, Compaq, Toshiba, Hewlett Packard and Olivetti. They operated a similar model. They built PCs to standard specifications and then shipped them to dealers who sold to end-users. Michael Dell conceived a different model. He allowed end-users to specify the exact configuration they wanted (memory, disk size, special function cards, etc) and then built it to order. The Dell PC was then shipped direct to the customer who could get telephone support to help set it up. Because there was no inventory waiting in distribution channels Dell was able to operate with much lower stock levels than his competitors. In a world where components were continually falling in cost and improving in specification this was a huge advantage.

Geoff Bezos used internet technology to develop an entirely different model for book and CD distribution when he set up Amazon. The traditional book and CD retailers had high overheads in retail premises and inventories. They could not compete with Amazon's huge selections, slick search facilities, customized recommendations and fast deliveries.

ARM was launched in 1990 as a tiny microprocessor company competing with huge players like IBM, Intel and Motorola, which all designed and manufactured their own chips. ARM took a radically different approach. Sir Robin Saxby, the visionary CEO, quoted in an article in *Engineering and Technology* magazine published in July 2006, said 'We had very little money so our only hope of creating a global standard was to license the design to everybody – turning our enemies into our friends. That put ARM into a different space. It was our open licensing business model and the power of our connected community that was the most significant factor in changing the world.' By 2006 some

98 per cent of the world's mobile phones were using at least one ARM designed processor and hundreds of companies have licensed ARM designs (including Intel).

How could you change your business model to bypass your competitor completely and delight customers with a radically better service? One way to explore this topic further is covered next in 'Ask "Who killed our business?"'

16. ASK 'WHO KILLED OUR BUSINESS?'

We can broadly simplify innovations into two kinds – incremental and radical. Incremental innovations are improvements to current products, methods, processes, services, partnerships and so on. Customer complaints and suggestions are a good source of ideas for incremental improvements. So are the people who work in the organization. If you ask customers how your product could be better or if you ask employees how their job could made easier they will come up with plenty of proposals. Most organizations are good at incremental innovation — they make things better. However, very few organizations are good at radical innovations. As Gary Hamel puts it, businesses are good at getting better but poor at getting different. Christensen (2003) argues that it is very difficult for successful organizations to develop disruptive innovations that would threaten the basis of their success. Often they are put out of business when some smaller company develops a radically new technology. Which employee working in a booming telecoms company in the 1990s would have suggested that free voice-over internet telephony would be something they should develop? It took a start-up, Skype, to bring this radical idea to market.

How can you encourage your people to countenance radical innovations? One way is to run creativity sessions where the objective is to conceive them. Ask the question 'Who killed our business?' Get small teams to imagine entirely new business models that could deliver the benefits that your customers want. Each team has to present a scenario of a force so powerful that it could replace you or put you out of business. Starting with a blank piece of paper and none of the encumbrances that limit your organization each team designs a super competitor. Teams are encouraged to go to extremes and to think completely outside the current model. The exercise is stimulating and can be very revealing.

Start by talking about examples of businesses that were wiped out. People come up with examples — ice supply companies that were eliminated by the refrigerator, carriage companies replaced by cars, music companies threatened by internet downloads, bookstores killed by Amazon and so on. As well as the impact of new technologies look at other forces such as fashion, demographics, routes to market and competition. We might consider what has happened to Arthur Anderson, Enron, Polaroid, PanAm and McDonalds. Then the teams have to think up a variety of forces that could put your organization out of business. They have to conceive entirely new ways of delivering the end-user benefits that they currently supply. When they have a good selection of possibilities they select the most potent force and work up a description of how it would work in practice.

When this exercise was conducted with a systems integration and consultancy company one team proposed a scenario where all their proprietary methods became available in the public domain. They went further by describing the idea of an internet business based in India delivering most of their consultancy value. A team from a major education establishment conceived how a collaborative venture involving Microsoft, Harvard Business School and a satellite TV company could replace them with a slicker multimedia operation.

Once the teams have chosen a business model that could kill them they have some further questions to ponder. If this is possible what should we doing about it? What is the ideal vehicle to develop and deliver this new business model? If this is coming should we start it ourselves, buy a business, adapt our methods or take some other action?

Most organizations have natural defence mechanisms against disruptive or threatening ideas. People immediately find reasons why they should not be considered. It is difficult to change the culture to one where such ideas are not only heard but are actively encouraged and developed. Asking the question 'Who killed our business?' is a good way to start.

17. LOOK FOR NEW WAYS TO REACH THE CUSTOMER

Many great business innovations started as new ways of reaching customers. In the late 19th century people living in the rural United States had to go into town to their local store to buy the goods they needed. The selection was poor and the items were expensive. A young railway company agent, Richard Sears, decided to try a new approach. Together with a watchmaker, Alvah Roebuck, he set up a mail order catalogue – initially offering watches and jewellery but expanding over the years to include a vast array of goods. They used the railroad and post office networks to deliver goods. The catalogues were novel, exciting and appealing to clients. Sears Roebuck became the world's largest retailer.

In 1886 David McConnel found a new way to sell cosmetics. His sales agent, Mrs P F E Albee, was the first Avon Lady. Using a network of women sales agents to sell directly to women in their homes, Avon grew rapidly. By 1928 Avon had 25,000 representatives. Avon has continued to grow and to empower women. It has more women in management positions (some 85 per cent) than any other Fortune 500 company. It is estimated that 90 per cent of American women have at some time bought something from Avon.

In 1959 two High School friends, Jay Van Andel and Richard DeVos, founded a company called Amway, an abbreviation for 'American Way.' They developed an innovative sales approach based on multi-level marketing networks. They sold a concept of owning your own business to people who sold their products and they convinced people to convince their friends of the benefits of the business model. It grew exponentially. The products were incidental; the network sold the model of the network. It is now a multi-billion dollar corporation with over 3 million business owners operating in 80 countries.

In the early 1990s Microsoft dominated the PC software market with their desktop packages sold through distributors, dealers and retail outlets. Anyone trying to sell a new software package faced huge barriers to entry. A little company called

Netscape found a way to bypass the traditional channels by offering their browser product, Navigator, as a free download on the internet. They charged for professional and developer versions. At the time it was a revolutionary way to distribute software. Netscape became leaders in the browser market.

We tend to think of innovation in terms of new products and services but new routes to market can be far more effective means to gain competitive advantage. There is a new way to reach the customers you serve today and the customers you want to reach tomorrow. Spend some time focusing on this issue, brainstorm new routes to reach clients and new ways to sell. It could be the best innovation investment you make.

18. ANTICIPATE THE WAVE

Great business innovators often appear to have anticipated a trend. It seems that they must have been prescient in that they got into the right place at the right time and produced the product or service that people wanted next.

How can some people forecast the future and anticipate the unknown? The reality is that they do not. More likely they observe something that is already happening and see an opportunity in it. William Gibson said, 'The future has already happened, it is just unevenly distributed.'

What a minority of people are doing today the majority will be doing tomorrow. All you have to do is to find that minority. To do that you have to develop your skills at understanding trends. You do this by keeping an open mind and trawling many different inputs. Search the internet. Read blogs. Scan different magazines. Travel to other countries. Meet new people. Discover things outside your normal zone of expertise and interest.

Whenever you see a new trend ask yourself what this might mean. What are the secondary consequences?

The invention of the motor car meant that in many instances people could travel faster than by using other forms of transport. A secondary effect was that people lived further from their place of work and the suburbs expanded.

The light bulb replaced candles. It also replaced going to bed early. Now people could read books or go out in the evening on streets and to buildings that were well lit.

The internet linked computers together. Jeff Bezos saw that this meant that people could buy things much more easily and he launched Amazon. Pierre Omydar saw that it enabled communities to join together in auctions and he launched eBay.

For each new trend there will be follow-ons, consequences and changes that create opportunities and threats. Every time you see a change in your business world, play a little game of What if…? What if this becomes a big trend? What will the consequences be?

19. INNOVATE BY SUBTRACTION

We tend to think that the best way to innovate is to add new features to our products or services. What can we add that increases the appeal of our offering? This route can easily lead to extra cost, feature overload and customer fatigue. Sometimes a better answer lies in subtraction.

Michael O'Leary, the founder of Ryanair, looked at the business process of passenger flights and built a new model by subtracting all the frills that meant extra cost. He subtracted:

- Travel agents. Customers book direct over the internet, so the middlemen and their costs are cut out.

- Tickets. Customers show their passport and quote their reference number. Subtracting tickets saves costs.

- Allocated seating. Customers choose a seat when they get on the plane, just like on a train or bus.

- Free drinks and snacks. If customers want a drink they have to buy it.

- Customer care – Ryanair has one-tenth the number of customer care attendants per passenger mile compared to BA. If a customer has a complaint the answer is generally – 'Hard luck, but what did you expect with such a cheap flight?'

Curves is a chain of franchised fitness centres. It has been enormously successful by doing less than the many other fitness centres and gyms it competes with. It subtracted half its potential audience by excluding men. It removed the pools, spas, locker rooms and fitness equipment that women did not use. By focusing on the equipment and fitness programmes that women really want it has offered excellent value for money and gained a leading share in a crowded market.

What can you take away from your current business process in order to save cost and simplify operations? Can you unbundle your product into separate components? Can you strip out costs or processes that not all customers want? Can you bypass a middleman on the route to your customer – as Direct Line, Amazon and Ryanair did? Egg and First Direct offered online banking and made it cost effective by cutting out all the branches that burden the traditional banks.

Sometimes you can get the customer to do something that you do right now. The supermarket was a remarkable innovation in the 1920s. The key new idea was to get customers to serve themselves rather than having an assistant serve them. A modern updating of the idea is provided by IKEA. Not only do customers act as assemblers in putting the furniture together, they also act as store men in collecting the flat packs from the warehouse.

The whole do-it-yourself business was built on the back of getting individuals to do what tradesmen had done for them in the past. eBay has built a business that runs like clockwork by getting the clients to place their own adverts, hold their own stock, sell and then ship their own goods and give each other recommendations. It is a triumph of transferring services to clients.

Next time you face the challenge of how to refresh your product don't just think about adding new features or services. Think about what you can cut out of the process or product. How can you make things simpler, less costly and more appealing to customers?

20. LOOK FOR THE SOLUTION WITHIN THE PROBLEM

Two prisoners dug an 80-foot tunnel from their cell to escape from prison. Where did they hide the dirt?   This is one of the examples used by Roni Horowitz of the consultancy group SIT to show the advantages of a method called systematic inventive thinking (SIT).

The answer is that they hid the dirt in the tunnel. The prisoners stole nylon sacks from the prison bakery and each day they dug the tunnel and put the dirt into the sacks. At cell inspection times they pushed all the dirt bags back into the tunnel and tidied the cell. When the prisoners escaped the guards found a cell full of bags of dirt and an empty tunnel.

It is a good example of one of the principles of SIT – look for the solution within the problem or its environment. The prisoners had very limited resources – but one of them was the tunnel itself.

If we are given unlimited resources to solve a problem, then we can always come up with something — and often it is expensive and over-engineered. When we have to use the limited set of resources contained in the problem and its immediate environment we are forced to be more creative - and very often the result is a solution that is elegant, inexpensive and effective. Using the tunnel to hide dirt is a prime example.

At the end of the first Gulf War fires were raging out of control in the Kuwaiti oil refineries. What could be used to put them out? One answer might have been sand. But a better solution was found. The pipelines that were normally used to pump oil from the refineries were used to pump water to the refineries. By using an existing resource and reversing the flow the problem was overcome.

Engineers are accustomed to working in very constrained conditions. In the very early Volkswagen Beetle car there was a problem of how to provide the power needed for the windscreen washer. The ingenious solution that the engineers came up with was to use the air pressure from the spare wheel (which was in the front of the car) to power the water jet.

It is not just product engineers who can use internal resources in ingenious ways. In 2005 the IRA allegedly pulled off a major robbery at the Northern Bank in Belfast – they got away with £25 million in banknotes. How could the authorities catch the criminals or stop them using the proceeds of their crime? They came up with a clever idea using one of the resources in the problem – the stolen banknotes. They changed the currency in Northern Ireland and reprinted all bank notes. Anyone holding old banknotes had to bring them in to be changed – and that is a big problem if you are holding millions of stolen banknotes.

So how can you use this approach in your problem solving? One of the methods taught in SIT is to break the problem down into a chain of unwanted effects. Now consider in turn each element in the problem or its environment and say to yourself – this element can be adapted to stop one of the unwanted effects and to break the chain. Then come up with ideas. By rigorously and imaginatively applying this technique you will often find an inventive solution.

Here is a moral dilemma that was used as a test in a job interview. You are driving along in your two-seater car on a wild, stormy night. You pass a bus stop, and you see three people waiting for the bus:

a) An old lady who looks as if she is about to die.

b) An old friend who once saved your life.

c) The perfect man (or) woman you have longed to meet.

Knowing that there is room for only one passenger in your car, what would you do?

Many answers were given but only one candidate out of 100 gave what was judged the best answer. He made ideal use of the resources in the problem. This is what he said: 'I would give the car keys to my old friend, and let him or her take the lady to the hospital. I would stay behind and wait for the bus with the woman of my dreams.'

There is an old saying, 'If life serves you lemons, make lemonade.' Use what you have got to best effect before complaining about your limited resources. The next time you face a tough problem do some lateral thinking. Try looking first at how you can use the resources in and around the issue. The solution could well be hidden somewhere inside the problem.

21. ASK 'WHAT IF...?'

Creative people use lateral thinking to test the boundaries of situations and challenge conventional approaches. Many of the idea generation techniques already considered use elements of lateral thinking to stimulate fresh lines of attack.

What if...? is a possibility thinking technique that can be used for problem analysis and exploration as well as idea creation. In the What if...? exercise every dimension of the question is tested with What if...? questions. The more ridiculous and provocative the questions the better. Say, for example, we are running a creativity workshop for a medium-sized company with 10 sales people and 200 customers. The challenge is 'How can we double sales?' The sort of what if questions we could ask might be:

- What if we had only one customer?
- What if we had 1 million customers?
- What if we had an unlimited marketing budget?
- What if we had no marketing budget?
- What if our products were free?
- What if our prices were three times what they are today?
- What if our salespeople could set their own commissions?

The question 'What if we only had one customer?' might suggest that we would have to give outstanding service to that customer and meet a range of needs we do not address today. This can prompt all sorts of ideas. Similarly if we had 1 million customers we would have to find new ways to service them – maybe using internet or automatic software routines rather than face-to-face contact. Each question prompts ideas and tests the rules and boundaries that are assumed to apply to the problem.

Start with the problem, generate a list of 20 or more 'What if...?' provocative questions. Then take these one at a time and use them to generate creative ideas. What are the consequences of the What if...? What would we do under these circumstances? Analyse and evaluate the resulting ideas. Some will lead to fresh insights. The process works best if people are really extreme and outrageous in the 'What if...?' stage.

22. PASS THE PARCEL

Pass the parcel is a powerful idea generation technique. It is quick, it is fun, and it generally delivers several good radical ideas. If your brainstorm meetings are turning up routine incremental ideas try this method to generate some really creative proposals.

It works well with groups of between four and eight people. Each person takes a blank sheet of paper and writes the challenge at the top. Then working silently and individually each person writes a completely crazy, bizarre and impossible solution to the question. No reasonable ideas are allowed at this stage; they have to be ridiculous. Each person then passes his or her sheet of paper to the person on their left. Now everyone has to use the idea in front of them as a springboard for a wild idea. This idea should be different from but triggered by the first idea. The sheets are then passed silently again to the left. Each person now has a piece of paper in front of him or her with two crazy ideas written on it. Each person has to use these to construct an outlandish but workable idea – one that is outrageous but feasible given enough resources. The sheets are passed again and now each person has to use the ideas to construct a novel but workable idea; one the person could propose to his or her peers. Each person in turn reads out the four ideas on his or her sheet – usually to peals of laughter. The group then analyses all the final ideas and chooses one or two – or synthesizes some of the ideas together to come up with a proposal.

For example, the challenge for a mobile phone company was 'How can we get all our employees to be evangelists for our products?' Here were four ideas as written in sequence on one sheet:

- Whenever our people see someone using a competitor's phone they snatch it from the person and smash it on the floor.

- When we see someone using a competitor's phone we snatch it from the person and give the person one of our phones free.

- Every employee has to persuade 10 strangers a month to try our phones.

- Every employee has vouchers for a special introductory offer for our phones. Employees give these to friends and people they meet. Every month whichever employee has the most vouchers redeemed gets a holiday for two.

This exercise is good fun and often generates very imaginative ideas. It involves silent individual action followed by group hilarity and discussion. It therefore makes a good change from the exercises that involve the whole group together all the time.

Pass the parcel can be operated as a three-step or four-step process. The Pass the Parcel three-step form is shown below.

The challenge:

---

1. A **bizarre, ridiculous, impossible** idea:

2. A **wild, outrageous but possible** idea triggered by the idea above:

3. A **creative, workable solution** based on the ideas above:

Figure 2   Pass the parcel

23. LOOK FOR A DISTANT RELATION

Most businesses look for new opportunities in the obvious places. They typically ask two questions:

Into what new markets can we sell our existing products or services?

What new products or services can we sell to our existing customers?

These are perfectly valid questions. You should ask them and explore the possibilities the answers bring. But don't stop there. If you do you may miss other and more exciting possibilities. Look for some distant relations as well as close cousins.

Caterpillar was a well-established leader in heavy earth-moving equipment. Then in 1996 the company started selling 'Cat' branded work boots. These were successful with young consumers who would never use or buy heavy Caterpillar machinery. By 2000 the company was selling over 25 million pairs of boots. It has now branched out into other kinds of clothing and toys to exploit the Cat brand.

Disney Corporation was a leader in cartoon films before it made the bold choice to go into theme parks. There were some synergies but it was not exactly an adjacent space in the market. The move was a great success and Disney subsequently branched into other areas such as musical shows (eg The Lion King) and stores selling related Disney products.

Richard Branson's Virgin Group takes this principle to extremes. The group deliberately breaks the marketing rules about only choosing adjacent markets or products. Virgin, having started in music, has launched companies in airlines, trains, banking, cola, wines, bridal wear and more. Indeed Richard Branson has founded over 200 separate companies. The only thing they have in common is the brand image of aggressive innovators and upstarts.

How can you find distant relations? Watch out for unexpected customer orders or compliments. Look for skills, strengths, extra services or by-products that your business has today but is not commercializing. Ponder what you are really good at. What is it that you can get passionate about? Ask employees and customers for ideas and suggestions. Above all, keep an open mind as regards possibilities.

24. IDEALIZE THE ANSWER

When you are looking at a tricky problem try specifying the ideal answer in a world where there are no constraints. What would a perfect solution look like if we had unlimited resources to achieve it?

Ackoff, Magidson and Addison (2006) describe how Bell laboratories did just such a thing with the telephone. In the 1950s the VP of Bell laboratories challenged teams of engineers to design 'the telephone system with which we would replace the existing system if we were free to replace it with whatever system we wanted.' The only constraint was that their designs be technologically feasible – ie no science fiction. The teams developed their designs and in doing so anticipated every change in the telephone system that has appeared since then, except two. Among the design criteria they specified were touch-tone phones, consumer ownership of phones, call waiting, call forwarding, voice mail, caller ID, conference calls, speaker phones, speed dialling and mobile phones. They did not anticipate photography by the phone or an internet connection. They were thinking 20 to 50 years ahead of their time and many of their ideas could not be realized until technology advanced and became affordable. However, many of their concepts were possible even in the 1950s and they put them into immediate action. One big innovation that came directly from this exercise was the touch-tone phone, which generated millions for AT&T in time saving on calls.

Staff at a major bank looked for an ideal solution for clients' needs. Someone asked the question, 'What if banks were open 24 hours a day, 7 days a week?' From this discussion emerged the idea of automatic telling machines (ATMs) – to give customers access to their accounts and money 24/7. Keeping banks open all the time was part of the original ideal solution but it was very expensive. A better answer was to create ATMs.

Try a blue sky session in which your team conceives the ideal solution for your client's requirements. Ignore the obstacles that are stopping you right now and imagine a perfect world where you can do anything except break the laws of physics.

List the key ideas and attributes of the ideal solution. By focusing on the epitome rather than the obstacles we can conceive all sorts of wondrous possibilities. When we start to examine these in more detail we often find that seemingly insuperable barriers can be overcome or worked around.

25. BE CAREFUL WHAT AND HOW YOU REJECT

Any suggestion scheme worth its salt will generate a large number of ideas – millions in the case of a company like Toshiba. In addition you will have ideas coming into the funnel from idea events and other sources. Obviously not every idea can be funded, developed and implemented, so many will have to be rejected. There is a tendency to accelerate this process by rejecting all outrageous ideas quickly so as to move on to the safe, steady, incremental ideas. But it is worth remembering what Einstein said, 'If at first an idea is not absurd, then there is no hope for it.'

Shell's famous Gamechanger programme is designed to encourage 'non-linear' ideas. Employees can submit ideas they think will result in increased revenues for Shell and the ideas are reviewed initially by a panel of their peers – not senior managers. If the idea looks promising experts review it and can immediately grant funding and skilled resource to enable the originator to build a prototype or develop a business case. One of the criteria that the evaluators have to use is: How much would Shell lose if we rejected this proposal and it turned out to be everything that its proposer says it will be? By considering the downside of missing out on a radical idea the risks and doubts are put into context.

Ideas that are rejected should be parked in a database so that they can be resurrected when input is needed. An idea that was rejected as unfeasible a year ago when oil was US $50 a barrel might be compelling when oil is US $200 a barrel. The old rejected ideas can later prove to be useful stimulations for new ideas.

The way in which the rejection is communicated to the originator is important. Creative people are sensitive souls. They care about their ideas. It is essential that they receive proper feedback and know that their idea was carefully considered. They need to hear the reasons for its rejection. A brusque 'It did not fit our criteria' will not do. If the rejection is handled properly people will continue to contribute ideas. If the rejection is handled badly you may just have lost another source of future ideas.

26. WEAR SIX THINKING HATS

Six Thinking Hats is an excellent thinking tool created by Edward de Bono. It can be used in many situations ranging from council meetings to jury rooms. It is particularly useful for evaluating innovative and provocative ideas.

As de Bono points out, most of our thinking is adversarial. You put up an idea and I criticize it in order to test its strength. The prosecution and defence in a courtroom are good examples of adversarial thinking. So are the Government and Opposition parties in Parliament. The trouble is that adversarial thinking in business meetings can be entrenched and politicized. For example, the sales manager opposes an idea because it came from the marketing manager. Both parties then dig in to reinforce their positions. Also people can be inhibited from criticizing ideas their boss puts forward.

The Six Thinking Hats technique overcomes these difficulties by forcing everyone to think in parallel. As they wear each hat they all have to think a certain way at the same time. Here is how it works when used for proposal review. The proposal is read out and then everyone puts on the following hats in turn:

- The white hat. This is the information hat and people can ask for more information or data to help analyse the proposal.

- The red hat. This hat represents emotions. People have to say how this proposal makes them feel emotionally. For example, some might say they feel threatened or scared by this idea. Others might say they feel excited. It is important to get the feelings expressed, as they can be hidden reasons why people would oppose or support a proposal.

- The yellow hat. This hat is the optimism hat. Everyone in turn has to say what is good about the proposal. Even if you hate the idea, you have to find some redeeming qualities and good points about it. All the benefits are listed and the most important are prioritized.

- The black hat is the hat of pessimism. Everyone has to find fault with the idea. Even if it was your idea and you are very proud of it, you have to point out some drawbacks. All the disadvantages are listed and the top ones prioritized.

▦ The green hat is the hat of growth and possibilities. Everyone has to suggest ways in which the idea could be adapted or improved to make it work better. It is good to have the yellow and black hat results in view here. A good sort of green hat question is 'How can we mitigate the key black items (disadvantages) and still get the main yellows (benefits)?' The green hat is the brainstorming hat. You use it to freely contribute suggestions.

▦ The blue hat is the process hat. It is used to review the thinking processes. You wear it when you discuss how you are using the method.

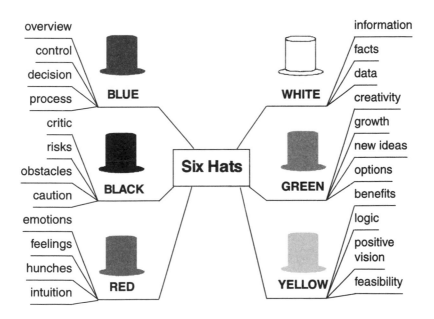

Figure 3   The Six Hats

Generally in the exercises you will spend fairly little time with the blue hat. The group will spend some time with the white and red hats but most time with the yellow, black and green hats. You can go back and forth from one hat to another, but the key rule is that everyone must wear the same hat at the same time. It is good to have a chairperson who holds up a coloured card or turns over a coloured cube to show which hat is in use and to make sure everyone is on board. If the chairperson sees someone using black hat thinking during the yellow hat session that person must be brought back into line.

The method is simple to run and remarkably effective in quickly and productively analysing proposals. It can also be applied in many other areas of business. If you want to use this method de Bono's book on the subject (2000) is highly recommended.

Section 4:
Implementing innovation processes

1. ALLOCATE TIME AND RESOURCES FOR INNOVATION

One of the commonest barriers to innovation is lack of time. People are just too busy doing their day job to spend time on trying new things. The common assumption is that working hard and working long hours are good things. Focus on delivering this quarter's results is the mantra.

It is as though we are so busy building rafts to cross the river that we never look up to consider building a bridge, or a tunnel or a dam or fording the river or building boats or planes or all the other things we could do. We just focus on producing those rafts.

If you want people to be creative, set the goal (crossing the river) and then challenge them to come up with ideas. Then give them time and some resources to test their ideas – to build prototypes, or to investigate what people elsewhere are doing.

Google allows its people to spend one day a week on innovative ideas. Is this a wasteful luxury? No. It has led to innovations such as Google Earth, Froogle and Gmail, which have generated hundreds of millions of dollars in extra revenues. Genentech has a similar provision for its people.

For many years 3M has allowed its scientists and engineers to spend up to 15 per cent of their time on any project that interests them. They do not have to ask their manager's permission but they do have to keep the manager informed of what it is they are doing. This permission to be free has resulted in countless ideas and innovations for 3M, which is regularly rated as one of the most innovative companies.

The message is clear. The leader has to free time for innovation in order to empower people to come up with great ideas and to explore them. Whether it is one day a week or one day a quarter, time for innovation is critical.

2. GIVE EVERYONE TWO JOBS

Give all your people two key objectives. Ask them to run their current jobs in the most effective way possible and at the same time to find completely new ways to do the job. Encourage your employees to ask themselves: 'What is the essential purpose of my role? What is the outcome that I deliver that is of real value to my clients (internal and external). Is there a better way to deliver that value or purpose?' The answer is always yes, but most people never even ask the question.

Being busy, efficient and effective is essential. It is necessary – but it is not sufficient. What is needed in addition is a restless hunger to find better ways to do things. Challenge people to find those better ways. Encourage executives to investigate how their kind of role is fulfilled in organizations in other fields. They could join industry associations and networks to learn about new and different methods. When someone finds a better way to do something that makes their own job obsolete praise and promote them.

You could add something like this to people's objectives:

Investigate and identify entirely new ways to achieve your goals.

Advise at least two radical alternative approaches in the coming year.

Make sure that such objectives are evaluated seriously at appraisal time.

3. IDENTIFY THE NEED FOR REPLACEMENT

The great management guru Peter Drucker said, 'Every organization must prepare for the abandonment of everything it does.' Think about your company today. Now think about what it might look like in 10 years' time. If it has survived, then nearly everything about it will have changed – in particular the products, the services, the methods, the processes and the business model. That is the inevitable outcome of the march of technology and competition. So why wait for the future to overtake you? Anticipate the trend and identify what needs to be replaced.

Most companies do this with their products. They have a development road map. It shows how the main sources of product revenue today will be replaced by new products – enhancements, replacements or radical diversions into new areas. Few companies do this with their systems, methods and work practices.

List all your current systems – in accounting, customer records, planning, marketing, sales, development, etc. Knowing that they will have to be replaced sooner or later, ask yourself: 'Which of these can we replace with something that will give us a real competitive advantage? How can we harness the latest technologies and thinking to leapfrog the competition?'

It is silly to replace sound systems just for the sake of change. But eventually all systems run out of steam. The objective for which they were originally designed has changed. They are no longer well suited for the new purposes of the business. We are patching and adapting them to make do. Prioritize which systems you are going to change this year and next year. Keep doing this and you will keep the blade sharpened. The process of innovation involves abandonment and renewal. Plan them both.

4. BORROW WITH PRIDE

The problem you face right now, whether at work, at home or in your social life, is a problem that someone else has faced and solved. Why not harness their ideas?

Doctors had a problem with hypodermic needles. Patients were afraid of them. Children dreaded them. The pain the needles caused was not intense but it was unpleasant and it dissuaded many people from having important injections. So the doctors asked – Who else has this problem? Who else injects into people and has solved this problem? The answer was quickly given. Mosquitoes insert a tiny needle into people and extract blood. They carry the deadly malaria virus. They go about their deadly work without being felt. By studying how the mosquito stings its victims, scientists were able to develop a hypodermic needle that patients do not feel.

Mick Pearce is the architect who designed a retail building called the Eastgate Centre in Harare, Zimbabwe. He wanted to keep the building cool in the hot summers but he wanted to do this with minimum energy use. He studied how termites build their mounds which keep remarkably cool. He designed a natural cooling system mimicking the workings of a termite nest. The building uses one tenth of the cooling energy requirements of conventional buildings.

The scientific study of nature in order to copy its methods is called mimetics. Alexander Graham Bell was a practitioner of mimetics. He copied the workings of the human ear when he invented the telephone. The diaphragm in the ear became the diaphragm in the telephone.

A successful innovation in your business does not have to be an all-new invention. It just has to be something new to your business that is beneficial. Maybe everyone in Singapore is doing it but you are the first in Holland; maybe every consulting firm does it but yours is the first doctors' surgery to try it; maybe everyone in IT knows about it but no one in hairdressing; maybe lots of youngsters communicate this way but you are the first city councillor to do so.

Rob McEwen took over a run-down gold mine in Ontario, Canada, the Red Lake mine. He was certain that there were good reserves of gold in the mine but the problem was how to find them. He had plenty of geophysical and other data on the mine but gold production kept going down.

At a computer conference he happened to hear about the Linux operating system and how its success was based on its open source principle – anyone could see any of the code. Thousands of programmers around the world analyse, extend and develop Linux code. He decided to borrow this idea and apply it in the conservative world of gold mining. He published all the data about the mine on the internet and challenged people to predict where to drill for gold. His colleagues thought he was crazy – no one ever gave away all their mining data. But the internet competition he started, the Goldcorp challenge, was a great success. The winner used sophisticated fractal graphics software to analyse the data and accurately predict where to drill for gold. The output of the mine went up tenfold.

How can you borrow with pride? Here are some suggestions:

- Travel extensively and see what similar organizations to your own in different parts of the word do.
- Read about industries other than your own. In the newsagent pick up specialist magazines in fields you know little or nothing about.
- Ask customers and suppliers for ideas – especially on new applications in your business area.
- Watch competitors – especially those in remote markets.
- In your brainstorming exercises use similes (as described on page 59) that force you to find analogies for your problem.

The telecoms company Vodafone has an interesting segmentation on its customers. Like every other business it segments customers by revenue and margin. But it also segments customers by which ones it can learn the most from. Vodafone identifies the top 20 clients worldwide who are doing the most interesting things with mobile technology. It ensures that senior managers visit these customers and keep abreast of their latest applications and uses. Some of these clients are very small organizations but Vodafone knows that the ideas they can garner from them are very valuable. Who are your most innovative clients? Do you monitor and track them. Do you keep them close? Could you borrow some of their great ideas?

5. TRAIN FOR INNOVATION

How did your organization acquire its skills in quality, sales, marketing, people management, finance and all the other myriad competences that you use? You hired people with the skills, or you trained people so that they acquired the skills, or people learnt on the job. If you want to develop expertise in innovation the same approaches apply. You hire creative people. You train people in the cultural and procedural aspects of innovation. And people learn about innovation by practising it.

The main areas for training include:

■ problem analysis;

■ questioning;

■ listening;

■ idea generation;

■ managing brainstorms;

■ idea evaluation;

■ de Bono's Six Thinking Hats;

■ prototype development;

■ project gating;

■ project management.

Generic training courses are available and there is some benefit in mixing with people from other environments. Most organizations prefer to run their own in-house courses tailored to their needs and addressing their issues. The primary purpose of the training is to develop skills and teach methods that can be applied. However, a secondary benefit that is often overlooked is that the training can yield useful ideas or help evaluate difficult choices. In order to do this it is important to set out with the objectives of ensuring that the right issues are addressed and that the best ideas in the day are captured.

6. MEASURE PROGRESS

Once you have set top-level goals you need innovation metrics to measure progress and to assess the overall state of your innovation capability. Monitoring should include the following:

■ You should measure your ability to fill the pipeline by monitoring the number of new ideas being generated.

■ If you have a suggestions scheme, you can scrutinize how many submissions you get each month.

■ You should check the efficiency of your innovation evaluation process by monitoring how many ideas make it through the initial selection and into the next stage as projects.

■ You should check how many projects become prototypes and how many prototypes become new products. Of these how many are incremental new products or extensions of existing lines and how many are radical innovations?

Other useful metrics include:

■ What is the innovation cycle time, ie how long does it take for an idea to go from conception to implementation?

■ How many people are engaged in innovation activities?

■ How much money is the organization spending on innovation?

■ What is the projected value of the projects in the innovation funnel?

■ What is the return on investment (ROI) on the new products and services launched this year?

■ How does the actual return compare with the original projected return on these projects?

7. BROADCAST SUCCESS

When you have successful innovations, be sure to broadcast the fact. Track the source of the original idea that led to the innovation. It may have come from a brainstorm meeting, a suggestion scheme item, an idea event or some other source and the originator may have been an individual or a team. In any event, if the contributor is agreeable, make a big fuss.

Draw up a story about the innovation and place it in internal and external media. Put it on your intranet and if appropriate on your main website. Place it in the trade press – journalists are usually hungry for stories and a good press release should ensure coverage. If at all possible feature the originators of the idea in the story with a photo of the person or people who came up with it.

Many managers prefer to keep their innovations secret for fear of giving away competitive advantage if the innovation works and for fear of humiliation if it flops. But generally the upsides outweigh the downsides. Broadcasting innovations sends a positive signal to the outside world about the company. Clients and prospective employees see this signal as well as competitors. But the biggest payback is internally. People feel good about seeing their name in print. Recognition is a powerful motivator and incentive. More ideas will flow and people will believe in the innovation process.

8. REWARD SUCCESS

Following on from broadcasting successful innovations you should reward the individuals who come up with good ideas.

The approach that was used in the past was to wait until as much as a year after an innovation was implemented, calculate the savings (on a very conservative basis) and then give the originator a fixed percentage (eg 10 per cent) of the savings. This led to occasional large payouts in manufacturing plants where someone spotted a way to cut cost significantly. But for most process improvements the cost savings were hard to measure and the wait for the reward was so long that people lost interest. Large payouts can also be divisive – especially when several people contributed to an idea but one person walks off with the bonus.

The more modern approach is to give many small incentives quickly. As soon as an idea is approved and enters the pipeline its originator gets a small reward. The idea may or may not emerge at the end of the funnel as a fully formed innovation, but the contributor is rewarded anyway. Instant gratification is the order of the day – all good ideas that gain initial acceptance are recognized.

Approaches for rewarding and recognizing innovative ideas and successful innovations include:

- giving gift vouchers;
- giving innovative gifts such as the latest mobile technical gadget.
- giving a voucher for dinner for two.
- holding an 'Innovation Oscars' – a gala awards ceremony where nominated finalists are feted and a winner is declared;
- featuring the winners in videos which are shown at annual innovation events;
- finding opportunities for people to attend foreign conferences.

Ideas are the lifeblood of innovation. Respond quickly to suggestions. Financially reward contributors. Implement the best ideas. Celebrate successful results.

9. TRACK THE ASTONISHING

There is a French construction company that uses an 'astonishment report'. Managers ask all new employees to complete the report at the end of their induction period. The employee must list anything he or she finds astonishing about the company – good or bad. It has to be done early – if employees waited 12 months to complete the report it would likely be too late. We only notice the astonishing when we first see it. After a while it becomes the norm.

The immigrant sees things that the citizen is blind to. And so it is with new employees, new clients and new suppliers. Things that surprise them seem normal to us, as in the view 'Doesn't everyone do it this way?'

The astonishment report can identify things that are surprisingly good, surprisingly bad or just odd about your company. It should prove particularly useful for those businesses that are successful and assume that they are doing most things right.

If you and your senior team have been with your organization for some time it is likely that you have blind spots. Try instituting an astonishment report to shine some light on these areas. You might be astonished at the results.

10. BE COOL OR OUTSOURCE COOL

Sometimes a staid organization needs an injection of external creativity. The internal innovation engine is just not producing enough power. Or the internal innovations are just not connecting with a young, fast-moving market. Sometimes a small agency can connect better with the clients than the company executives can. And sometimes the outsiders can find it easier to suggest risky things that the insiders dare not say or cannot conceive.

Hasbro is US $3 billion Toy Company with 6,000 employees. It has a number of leading and long-standing brands, including Transformers and My Little Pony. It wanted to refresh these lines, so it called in a tiny creative agency, Thunderdog Studios. What can Thunderdog bring that Hasbro does not already have? For a start, they bring a youthful outlook. As president Tristan Eaton says in an article by Lucas Conley in *Fast Company*, published in July 2006, 'We're waiting for them to realize we're just a bunch of kids.' The same issue of *Fast Company* looks at Strawberry Frog – a 'hipster ad shop' – an agency that specializes in bringing a cool look to clients' branding issues. The company's clients include eminent blue-chip companies like Time Inc and Mitsubishi.

Why do successful companies bring in such outside agencies? One reason is that it is very difficult to maintain a cool image – especially in a business where young consumers decide what is cool and what isn't. It requires a keen sense of what the new trends are, an ability to scan youth horizons and an ability to gamble on the next wave. Just as middle-aged parents have to ask their teenage children for advice on modern styles of music, dance or clothing, so it is with well-established companies.

Big companies can try to do this with internal resources. Procter & Gamble has a separate internal group called Tremor that tests new ideas, products and concepts with a network of 200,000 youngsters. Procter & Gamble have also launched a group called Vocalpoint to canvass the views and reactions of 600,000 mothers.

But for organizations that lack the resources of Procter & Gamble it may be worth employing an agency of 'kids' to tell your venerable executives what is perceived as cool and what is not.

11. COLLABORATE

Many CEOs now see collaboration as key to their success with innovation. They know they cannot do it all using internal resources. So they look outside for other organizations to partner with. A good example was previously quoted as a weird combination — Mercedes and Swatch, which collaborated to produce the Smart car. Each organization brought dissimilar skills and experiences to the team.

Costa Coffee is a chain of coffee shops in fierce competition with Starbucks and Café Nero in the UK coffee bar market. It has had considerable success by collaborating. Costa develops concessions with key partners. Current concession partners include Abbey National banks, W H Smiths and Waterstones book stores and Homebase DIY stores. According to Costa's website (www.costa.co.uk – accessed 2006) the con-cession stores are managed by the Costa team, who provide high-quality coffee and service experience to businesses that want to provide their customers with that little something extra. Customers in concession stores can relax with a cup of coffee and food offering as they take a break from retail therapy, consider that purchase or await an appointment.

The next step beyond collaboration is open innovation. This is something that Procter & Gamble, IBM and Kimberly-Clark have focused on as a way of driving innovation. Open innovation replaces the vertical integration of innovation processes within one company with a network of collaborators working on innovation projects. Using outsiders can speed up processes, reduce costs, introduce more innovative ideas and reduce time to market.

In an article in the *Dallas News*, published on 8 August 2006, Katherine Yung reported how Kimberly-Clark reduced the time it takes to bring out new products by 30 per cent through open innovation. It launched Sunsignals in just six months by collaborating with a smaller company, SunHealth Solutions. Sunsignals is a self-adhesive sensor that changes colour when the wearer is in danger of burning in the sun.

Procter & Gamble aims to source 50 per cent of its innovations from outside using open innovation. Early results include new products such as Mr. Clean Magic Eraser and Pringles Prints.

The same *Dallas News* article reported that in 2005 Kimberly-Clark partnered with more than 30 companies in joint development, joint ventures, co-distribution and licensing deals.

Here are some key steps for success in open innovation:

- Each party should define what it wants to get out of the relationship.

- It must be clear who owns the intellectual property in the partnership.

- Each side should allocate a senior person with overall responsibility for the success of the partnership.

- Key obligations, expectations and milestones should be established early.

- Each party should remember that honesty and trust is built on clear communication — especially when objectives look likely to be missed.

- A good legal contract should be in place.

12. OBSERVE CUSTOMERS

Customers can be an important source of innovative ideas. Many companies conduct conventional customer surveys and focus groups. These are useful channels of feedback, but in terms of original ideas they are often disappointing. Customers are good at demanding incremental improvements in products, lower prices and better service, but they are notoriously poor at predicting significant new products or innovations to meet their needs. Before the fax machine was invented who would have predicted he or she needed it? Which wearer of spectacles in the 1950s would have said that he or she wanted a lens to put on the eyeball or laser surgery to reshape the eye? You can expect customers to tell you that they want more of what you offer and they want it better, faster and cheaper. But do not count on them to tell you about different ways to meet their needs. A more lateral approach to gain insights from customers is to study in detail how they use your type of product or service and to observe what practical problems they have.

Fluke Corporation of Seattle is noted for innovative hand-held measurement products. The company sent teams of observers to watch maintenance engineers in chemical plants. The observers discovered that the engineers had to carry a variety of different instruments to calibrate different temperature and pressure gauges. They also noticed that after taking the calibration measurement the engineer would write the readings on a clipboard and then transcribe them into a computer. The process was time-consuming and prone to errors. Fluke therefore designed a new product that used flexible software to allow it to calibrate any gauge in the chemical plant. It also recorded the results, which could be directly downloaded to the engineer's computer. The resulting product was the Fluke Document Process Calibrator, which became a great success.

Haier is a leading Chinese manufacturer of white goods such as freezers and cookers. Its engineers in rural China were surprised to find that people were using Haier washing machines to wash the vegetables they had grown in their gardens. Turning this unexpected use into a new application, the Haier development team came up with a new wash cycle designed specifically for vegetables. On another occasion a sharp-eyed engineer saw that a student had placed a plank between two Haier fridges to form a makeshift desk. The company responded by designing a fridge with a fold-out desktop – ideal for small rooms that need an extra table or desk top.

Asking customers for feedback is good but observing them can be much better. If you want to gain a march on the competition and design the products and services of the future, watch your customers carefully. Look for the areas of unexpected use, the headaches and problems that want to be solved or the unusual combinations of needs or uses. They can give you the insights you need to generate successful innovations in products, services and processes.

Many companies have a policy that senior executives have to spend some time each year working on the front line. Retailing executives work in a store. Bank directors serve at a counter. Insurance bosses go out with assessors. Hospital directors work on a ward. This 'dose of reality' has many advantages. Executives meet, serve and observe customers. It gives an up-to-date picture of what is happening at the sharp end of the business. It improves understanding of and sympathy with staff issues. Above all, it helps the executives see the many areas for improvement in operation and service. It has paved the way for many innovations.

13. CO-CREATE

Customers are a great source of innovation. Asking your customers gives you incremental ideas. Observing your customers can give you radical ideas. An increasingly powerful third route is co-creating with your customers.

Threadless is a fashion company that has had great success asking people to upload T-shirt designs that site visitors then rate each week. Winning submissions get printed in limited editions, and the creators are rewarded with US $750 in cash and US $250 in site credit. Those prizes aren't going to make anyone rich, except maybe Threadless, which can freely reprint successful designs. But the process does create opportunities. As Yuval Rosenberg reported in an article published in *Fast Company* in April 2006, when the company's founders needed to hire a graphic artist, they didn't have to look far. Ross Zietz, a 24-year-old from Baton Rouge, Louisiana, had won eight weekly contests. 'They saw what I was capable of through my work for the competitions', says Zietz, who had also been approached to design T-shirts by others who had seen his Threadless portfolio.

The same issue of *Fast Company* reported that Converse, a division of Nike, received more than 1,500 video submissions when it invited consumers to send in 24-second shorts inspired by Chuck Taylor shoes and the Converse brand. It has used 40 of the videos as TV spots, rewarding the creators with US $10,000 each.

An article by Gerhard Gshwandtner in *Selling Power*, published in October 2006, reports a similar initiative from Doritos, which invited consumers to create a 30-second commercial to sell Doritos. Online consumer voting in January 2007 picked the winners. Five finalists received US $10,000 each. The Grand Prize winner's commercial will be aired during the 2007 Super Bowl XLI.

Companies are exploiting the opportunities presented by the creative minds of their customers. For example, to celebrate its 150th anniversary, Timex conducted a global design competition: 'Timex2154: The Future of Time'. Designers from 72 countries explored the future of personal and portable time-keeping and sent in 640 surprisingly creative entries.

In the past, customers have been limited to communicating their wants and needs in surveys and focus groups; today, brands deploy existing technologies to map their customer's imagination. Brands no longer view consumers as targets with a wallet, but as co-creators of exciting and profitable solutions.

Why not throw down a challenge to your customers to help design your next range of products or services? Set a competition and reward the most imaginative ideas. Use internet, video, chat room or other technologies to allow your clients to express themselves.

14. CREATE A COMMUNITY

One great way to harness the collective creative power of your customers is to create an online community.

Wikipedia created an innovative product – an online encyclopaedia – by garnering a community of contributors who built all the articles. It is an open source creation. All sorts of people post contributions and the community can organize, correct and manage itself – like some huge living organism. The content of the Wikipedia encyclopaedia is not as accurate as conventional works but some might say that it makes up for this in its immediacy, accessibility and breadth.

Myspace fashioned a valuable and unorthodox product with a community for youngsters and their music. It became wildly popular with teenagers who enjoyed creating their own pages and listening to new and trendy bands. Youtube did something similar by allowing users to post their home-made videos. It grew massively with hundreds of millions of visits per day as people shared cool and funny video clips.

All of these sites and many more have benefited from user generated content. The site owner provides the structure but the users provide the content and the value. How can you do something similar for your stakeholders – whether customers, suppliers, or employees? Ask yourself these questions:

- What shared interests or concerns do these people have?

- What specialist knowledge would they be prepared to share?

- How can we add value to the process?

Many organizations use blogs to approach these issues and that is a good starting point provided the blog gives value and impartiality rather than publicity and the company's viewpoint. The next step is to create an online community that generates its own worth. The risk is that it cannot be controlled. The upsides are many – you will be seen as cool and helpful, the online community will attract new visitors to your area; it will generate a tremendous number of new ideas, concerns, issues and initiatives. Some of these could lead to suggestions for new products or services you could offer.

If you want a fruitful topic for a brainstorm meeting ask: How can we create a community for our users?

15. CROWDSOURCE

A powerful way to gain innovative solutions to tough problems is to crowdsource. The term was coined to describe the process of outsourcing an issue or problem to an independent 'crowd' of experts who compete (or sometimes collaborate) to solve the problem. They are usually rewarded handsomely for doing so.

Wu Jiazhi, a student at Zhejiang University in China, became a big winner in programming contests offered by Topcoder Inc, a company that works with the likes of America Online and Merrill Lynch. Clients approach Topcoder with tough software problems and Topcoder invites programmers from around the world to solve these problems over the internet. Within weeks of entering his first contest, Wu had bagged US $2500, which he used to buy his first laptop. Since then he has earned over US $200,000 from Topcoder (as reported in an article published in *Business Week* published on 6 November 2006).

Innocentive (www.innocentive.com), a company founded by Eli Lilley in 2001, is a marketplace for science problems and solutions. Top companies like Procter & Gamble, Boeing and Dupont post tough science problems on the site. A community of over 100,000 scientists from around the world compete to come up with solutions to the problems and can earn prizes of as much as US $1million.

It is clear that you do not have to rely on an in-house R&D department to solve all your technical problems or to come up with technical innovations. You can outsource this function and pay only for results. You can crowdsource your way to technical innovations.

16. GATE THE PROCESS

Many larger organizations use a formal gating process to manage their innovation pipeline. This is usually based on the Stage-Gate® methodology developed by Bob Cooper (www.stage-gate.com, 2006). The diagram used on the Stage-Gate website is shown below.

Stage-Gate® Product Innovation Process

Figure 4

A Stage-Gate process is a conceptual and operational roadmap for moving a new-product project from idea to launch. Stage-Gate divides the effort into distinct stages separated by management decision gates. Cross-functional teams must successfully complete a prescribed set of related cross-functional tasks in each stage prior to obtaining management approval to proceed to the next stage of product development (www.stage-gate.com/knowledge_pipwhat.php 2006).

Stages are:

■ Where the action occurs – the project team completes key activities to advance the project to the next gate.

■ Cross-functional – (there is no R&D or marketing stage). Each activity is undertaken in parallel to accelerate speed.

■ Where risk is managed – vital information (technical, market, financial and operations) is gathered to manage risk.

- Incremental – each stage costs more than the preceding one, resulting in incremental commitments. As uncertainties decrease, expenditures are allowed to rise and risk is managed.

Gates are:

- where the Go/Kill and prioritization decisions are made;
- where mediocre projects are culled out and resources are allocated to the best projects;
- focused on three key issues: quality of execution; business rationale; and the quality of the action plan.
- where scorecards and criteria are used to evaluate the project's potential for success.

The process is popular and well-proven as a means of speeding the development process for new products and initiatives.

It is easy to become obsessed with getting projects through the gates – where the approvals are made. But the real progress is made in the stages – that is where the value is added. As Allan Ryan of Managed Innovation International Pty Ltd puts it in 'Innovation Tools, Innovators share the lessons they've learned in 2005' (www.innovationtools.com), 'Better projects, better thinking and better execution are created in the STAGE and ensure that GATE targets are not just met but exceeded.'

If you want to develop and manage a pipeline of product innovations, then the Stage-Gate process is recommended. Read more about at it at www.stage-gate.com.

17. APPOINT INNOVATION CHAMPIONS

Getting innovative ideas though the morass of decision-making processes in a large organization is difficult. Changing a complacent, conservative culture to an entrepreneurial one is even harder. The innovative leader cannot do it all by himself or herself. He or she needs a cadre of trusted allies in each department – the innovation champions.

Even if everyone buys into the vision and goals of innovation they easily slip back into their old ways. Innovation champions are people who are charged with making innovation happen at a grass roots level. They are senior people - but not necessarily department heads. They track the innovation pipeline in their area. They encourage the sponsors of promising innovation initiatives. They smooth obstacles and help secure approvals. They network across the organization and with other innovation champions. They stay aware of what is happening in other departments and outside the business.

Ultimately the goal is that innovation champions will work themselves out of a job. Ideally everyone is committed to innovation, the process works smoothly and there is no need for a 'Mr Fix it'. Until that happens, having someone with the enthusiasm, drive and political clout to make innovation happen is critical.

18. RUN AN INNOVATION INCUBATOR

The toy company Mattel is well known for its Barbie doll brand. It needs a constant stream of internal innovations to build on this success. So Ivy Ross, Senior VP of Girls Toy Design, set up something she called Project Platypus. The idea is based on the description of a platypus as an uncommon mix of different species. The 12 members of the project team are a rotating group drawn from different functions in the company. They join the project for three months and work intensely and creatively. Operating in a dramatically different environment, they use external stimuli, study children at play and have enormous freedom to generate and test ideas. The participants enjoy the experience and take their new creative skills back to their departments. The results have been startling, with many new products and reduced time to market. As Ivy Ross says, 'Designers are not the only people who can create toys. If you put a bunch of creative thinkers in the right environment and drop the job titles, you'll discover amazing creativity' (from an article in *Fast Company* entitled 'Ivy Ross is not playing around', published in November 2002).

To develop winning products, Samsung, the Korean electronics company isolates artists and 'techies' for months on end. Because daily routines can interrupt the flow of great ideas, Samsung segregates development teams in its VIP (Value Innovation Programme) Centre. Product planners, designers, programmers and engineers are asked to outline the features and design of new products such as the company's mainstay flat-screen TV. Department heads pledge to keep staff posted there until they have completed the assignment.

The facility is a sort of boiler room where people from across the company brainstorm day after day – and often through the night. Guided by one of 50 'value innovation specialists', they study what rivals are offering, examine endless data on suppliers, components, and costs, and argue over designs and technologies.

By bringing together everyone at the very beginning to thrash out differences, the company believes it can streamline its operations and make better gadgets. The centre, at Suwon, Samsung's main manufacturing site, 20 miles from Seoul, is open 24 hours a day. Housed in a five-story former dormitory, it has 20 project rooms, 38 bedrooms, a kitchen, a gym, traditional baths, and ping-pong and pool tables. In one year some 2,000 employees cycled through, completing 90 projects. Products that have come out of the centre include a notebook computer that doubles as a mobile TV, yet is thin and light enough to be carried in a handbag, and the CLP-500, a colour laser printer that was built at the same cost as a black-and-white model.

Every step of the way, team members drew what Samsung calls 'value curves'. These are graphs that rank various attributes such as picture quality and design on a scale of 1 to 5, from outright bad to excellent. The graphs compare the proposed model with those of rival products and Samsung's existing TVs (reported in an article entitled 'Camp Samsung') published on 3 July 2006 in *Business Week*.

By deliberately forcing the mixing of project teams and removing distractions Mattel and Samsung speed up the innovation process. People in the teams are encouraged to be creative and to break the rules. They focus on getting the innovation moving. And they bring cooperation, enthusiasm and diversity to bear on the problem. An incubator can overcome the problems of corporate inertia and inter-departmental fault-lines by concentrating the resources of people, skills and time needed to deliver new products.

19. EMPLOY AN IDEAS SEARCHER

Bristol Myers Squibb is one of the world's largest pharmaceutical companies. One of the employees has the title 'ideas searcher'. Her job is to source ideas for challenges that people bring to her. She might run a brainstorm meeting, an intranet competition, look outside or inside but she will find some great ideas for your problem.

In a typical year she will run 20 to 30 different major idea generation campaigns. For example, when the patent on the drug Glucophage was about to expire she ran a campaign to find ways to promote sales. She organized employees to walk around wearing sandwich boards saying 'We're fighting diabetes and we need your help.' She solicited ideas from staff at meetings and over the intranet. Over 4,000 ideas were generated and over 400 were seriously evaluated (Tucker, 2002: 126).

Having someone whose job it is to drive idea generating programmes can liberate creative thinking and drive innovation. That person can select from a variety of techniques to put together an energising campaign for any big topic. The original sponsor may feel inhibited about running some crazy events and in any case he or she is too busy to give the programme the time that is needed. The ideas searcher can devote the time and energy to make it happen.

20. STREAMLINE YOUR APPROVAL PROCESS

Draw a flow chart diagram of your organization's approval process for innovations. Pick an example for a theoretical new idea. Suppose it is a good idea to improve customers' satisfaction that would involve significant spending and the cooperation of several departments. What levels of approval and authority would it need to see the light of day? Who are the key stakeholders in the approval process? Who has the right of veto? What levels of planning or business case development are needed to get it through the system?

Draw as detailed a flow chart as you can showing the Go/No go decision points and the feedback loops where ideas are sent back for reconsideration. Now ask some questions. Is this process fit for purpose? Is it over-engineered? Are there too many hurdles for new proposals to jump? Often when this exercise is done we find that the approval process has been designed for significant new product initiatives but it is unwieldy for smaller developments or process improvement proposals that still have to jump through all the hoops.

The National Audit Office in the UK examined innovation in the government sector and found that approval processes were inappropriate and deterred innovation. Here are some of the report's key findings (National Audit Office, 2006):

Government departments and agencies should ensure that:

▪ Their review processes are purposeful and proportionate for the risks that the innovations pose.

▪ Pilots are appropriately scaled for projects and analysed.

▪ Reversible innovations can be tested speedily and at small scale before being rolled out more widely.

▪ Decision-making processes take appropriate account of the opportunity costs of delays, especially the foregoing of expected financial savings.

These recommendations apply to large organizations everywhere.

21. KILL THE LOSERS

How are you going to find the resources you need for the promising projects? One great way is to kill off the failing projects. Many organizations find this difficult to do. Consequently the creative ideas they generate are always short of money and manpower.

The problem is that once a promising project starts it can be very hard to stop. People become committed to it and are reluctant to 'waste the effort we have already put in'. That is why the gating process is so important and the criteria have to be enforced. Many companies find this difficult. They lack the processes. They do not know exactly what resources they have deployed and the project managers cling to failing or marginal projects.

Egos, empire and politics muddy the waters. Projects that are interesting and have some potential benefit keep going because of the resources that have already been invested. It is the 'we can't stop now' syndrome. But the key question is this: is this the best use of these resources right now? Although the project may be beneficial, if it is blocking the implementation of a project with a significantly higher payback, then it should stop. You have to be ruthless in weeding out the sickly plants so that the best specimens can flourish.

22. BUILD PROTOTYPES

How do you get people to buy into an idea? How can you help them to really grasp the concept, understand what it is and to make suggestions rather than criticisms? One of the best ways is to make it real. Build a prototype.

Tom Kelley of IDEO says this about how Jeff Hawkins of Palm developed the Palm V PDA to replace the rather clumsy Palmpilot:

> From the outset, Hawkins approached the Palm V as a verb and not a noun. He carried a crude wooden prototype around in his pocket, even pulling it out during meetings to simulate the taking of notes or checking of his calendar. Whether he realised it or not, he was beginning a process of exploration that was similar to what Art Fry, inventor of the Post-it note, engaged in when he handed out the little stickies to secretaries and fellow employees and watched his innovation take on a life of its own. (Kelley, 2002: 261)

That is all very well for a PDA or reusable sticky notes you might think – they are tangible products – but what if you have a service, how do you knock up a quick prototype of that? The answer is that you model it with role play. Let people see how the new service might work by having them play the role of the customer, or the consultant, or the service provider, or whoever is appropriate.

People misunderstand words. They find abstract concepts difficult to grasp. The innovation idea that is clear in your mind can be befuddled in theirs. Whenever possible create something they can see, touch and feel. Then they will make suggestions for how it could work better.

People's Bank has a refreshingly original attitude to new ideas. 'Don't debate it, test it' is one of the key philosophies of this innovative US financial services organization. As outlined in Allan *et al* (1999: 122), fed up with endlessly debating whether an idea was a winner or a loser and learning little along the way, the bank shifted its paradigm to a 'test it before you judge it' approach. The result is an organization dedicated to making new ideas real as quickly as possible and then piloting them in managed circumstances to check the appeal and improve the idea.

23. IMPLEMENT

As it is with prototypes so it is with production products. You should be looking to get something out there quickly.

Everything else in the innovation process is meaningless if you do not implement innovations. The whole purpose of all the creativity, the ideas, the pipeline, the prototypes and the stage gates is to produce implemented products, services or methods. Innovation only becomes real when something is put into operation.

There is a saying in business 'Ready, fire, aim.' Don't wait until you are sure that your aim is true – take your best shot and see what happens. Of course if you are making parachutes, or foodstuffs or pharmaceuticals, then you can't ship exploratory products that are not fully tested. But in many other fields you can.

The temptation is to test every possible bug out of the product, to plan its launch in minute detail and to protect it from view for fear of alerting the competition. We can easily get into 'paralysis by analysis', where we substitute planning for action. Planning and testing are essential, but their levels should be appropriate to the nature and risk of the venture.

The approach of People's Bank here is salutary. Their motto, 'Don't debate it, test it' applies to products as well as prototypes. It is similar to the motto that Sir Richard Branson uses at Virgin Group, 'Screw it, let's do it!'

If at all possible try the product at low cost in a section of the marketplace and see what the customer's reaction is. You will learn far more in the real world than you will in the test laboratory or with focus groups.

Innovation is a like the children's game of battleships. You try some speculative shots and see if you hit something. If you fail you move on and try somewhere else. If one of your shots hits something you focus there to see what it is you have hit – you find out how big the opportunity really is.

Your attitude to implementation is linked to your attitude to failure. If you are afraid of failure, then you will be reluctant to implement innovations. If you are comfortable with managing the risk of failure, then trying things in the marketplace is exciting. It is the best way to learn what works and what doesn't. Innovative leaders have a restless curiosity. They are anxious to be out there trying innovations and assessing real feedback from early users. 'Fail often and fail cheap' is their watchword. They implement innovation as quickly as they can. They kill off the losing products promptly. They reinforce winning innovations. They implement their way to success.

24. OVERCOME CUSTOMER RESISTANCE

Sometimes the biggest resistance to innovation comes from the person who should benefit most from it – the customer. Customers can be very conservative. When you come along with a great new product or service they are often initially unimpressed. Why should the buyers take a risk with your unproven new gismo? They know that new products often have bugs and they do not want to be the guinea pigs on which you experiment. The customers are familiar with the current method – why should they change?

This is understandable and needs careful handling. Your sales people will doubtless be adept at explaining the benefits of the innovation but the customers are right to be sceptical. You need to find ways to reassure them and to mitigate their risk.

At the same time you need early adopters so that you can get some traction in the market, customer feedback and positive references (we hope). So acknowledge the customers' concerns and put offers in place to allay those concerns. For example, you could:

- Allow customers a free trial of the new product.

- Continue to provide the old service so that they can go back to it at any time.

- Offer a money-back guarantee.

- Provide a special service level that gives them immediate access to your top support experts.

- Agree joint service level agreements.

- Stress the payback and benefits they will receive and even make payment dependent on their being achieved.

- Promise to arrange a positive PR result for them in the trade press if the trial succeeds.

Above all choose the right early customers – some people love new technology and others hate it. Select the best early adopters from among your top clients and then secure their personal testimonials when the product succeeds. You are in it together and it must be a win–win for both parties.

Section 5:
Building a creative culture

1. DON'T TELL, ASK

Innovative leaders have a restless curiosity. They are forever asking questions. They inculcate the same habit with their people.

In an article by Jeremy Caplan, published in *Time* magazine on 2 October 2006, Google CEO Eric Schmidt is quoted as saying:

> We run the company by questions, not by answers. So in the strategy process we've so far formulated 30 questions that we have to answer. What are the next big breakthroughs in search? And the competitive questions: What do we do about the various products Microsoft is allegedly offering? You ask it as a question, rather than a pithy answer, and that stimulates conversation. Out of the conversation comes innovation. Innovation is not something where I just wake up one day and say 'I want to innovate.' I think you get a better innovative culture if you ask it as a question.

Collins (2001: 60) says, 'One of the crucial elements in taking a company from good to great is somewhat paradoxical. You need executives, on the one hand, who argue and debate – sometimes violently – in pursuit of the best answers, yet on the other hand, who unify fully behind a decision, regardless of parochial interests.' We want our people to be questioning and yet supportive.

Everyone starts out on their first day in the organization by asking lots of basic questions. 'Why do we this?' 'What is the purpose of that?' and so on. As time goes by we stop asking the basic questions. We tend to assume that the way we do things is the natural, ordered way to do things. This thinking must be challenged. To build an innovative culture you need to ensure that everyone can ask questions and does ask questions.

Why do people not question things? There are three main reasons. The first has to do with comfort, complacency and even laziness. Why bother challenging how things are done when we are cruising along nicely? Secondly, people are just too busy to stop and ask why they are doing the things they are doing or whether there is a better way. It takes all their time and energy to get the job done. Thirdly, many people are afraid to ask basic questions for fear of looking foolish or of being upbraided by their manager for challenging him or her or questioning company policy.

Each of these issues must be addressed. Leaders at all levels must encourage people to ask questions and must welcome those challenges when they come. Many managers feel uncomfortable with this. They feel that once a company policy has been set everyone should conform and work hard to ensure its achievement. Of course this is to a large extent right. We do not want endless bickering. There is a time for action and there is a time for questioning. We must create occasions when any challenge is acceptable. We must also overcome the inhibitions that people harbour. There must be no ridicule, criticism or cynicism for genuine queries.

A good way to kill all three birds with one stone is to hold good brainstorm meetings (see pages 55–60). They give people time and space for questions and suggestions. They provoke unorthodox ideas and we welcome all questions – including challenges to any aspect of policy or direction. The rules of brainstorming preclude negativity, cynicism or criticism during the idea phase. Generate a culture where anyone can question anything in a constructive spirit. Kick off the process with some dynamic idea creation sessions using sound brainstorming techniques.

2. PRAISE THE INNOVATORS

If you want to change the culture of the organization, one of the best ways to do it is to praise the behaviours you want to see. If you want your people to be more adventurous, more entrepreneurial and more innovative, then make a point of singling out for recognition those people who are acting like that. Catch someone doing something good and make a fuss of them.

Say you have a culture that is risk averse, where people are reluctant to try new things for fear of failure. Find someone who tried something that did not work and then call that person out at an all hands meeting. 'John tried an experiment. Unfortunately it did not work. But do you know what? Trying things is exactly what we need here. I want to say well done to John for having the guts to push this prototype. We have learnt a valuable lesson. If we are going to be innovative we have to try more things and be ready to cope with some inevitable setbacks along the way. So let's have a big round of applause and hear it for John!'

This is much more powerful than praising those whose initiatives succeeded – though you should certainly do that too. By praising someone for failing you are sending a strong message that countervails the current culture.

At your next department meeting see if you can find someone to praise for:

- coming up with some great ideas;
- trying something new;
- challenging the conventional way of thinking;
- bringing an external idea into the company;
- collaborating with a different department or organization;
- taking a risk;
- making something happen.

Praise is one of the most powerful weapons in the leader's armoury. Make sure you use it effectively and often.

3. FOCUS ON WHAT WENT RIGHT

We tend to focus our attention on what went wrong. We try to fix problems. A typical management meeting consists of a group of people who are looking at what is not working and trying their hardest to come up with ways to put things right. But in the process they are often allocating blame, arguing, becoming negative and getting frustrated.

Most managers ask these kinds of questions:

- Why are sales down?
- What is holding up production?
- What can we do about customer complaints?
- What can I do about difficult staff?
- What is wrong with the current process?
- Where can we speed things up?
- How can we stop all these problems?

These are good questions and problems have to be addressed. However, by focusing our attention on the negative we miss the opportunities presented by the positive. We should spend some time asking questions like these:

- What are our key strengths?
- What do customers like about us?
- What is going well?
- What unexpectedly good things have happened here recently?
- What new customers have we won?
- In what ways have we delighted customers?

By focusing on our strengths and capabilities we can see positive opportunities. If we concentrate on fixing the current model, then we can easily miss new possibilities. All our energies are going into alleviating problems and weaknesses – this denies us the chance to create new initiatives.

It is the same with people. When we are toddlers everyone praises us and tells us how wonderful all the things we do are. Then as we go through the school process things change and the emphasis switches, the errors in our work are pointed out and teachers tell us all the things we could better. This is well meant but the impact on fragile egos can be severe.

When we get to work we are at first acutely aware of our lack of experience and authority. At our annual appraisal we are told the things we need to focus on to improve. We plan training and coaching to improve our weak areas. Our strengths are taken for granted and development focuses on our weaknesses in order to make us 'more rounded'.

But surely the key to success is to build on our strengths and to compensate for weaknesses. If someone has a good voice but can't dance, why would that person try to become an all-rounder? Why not try to become a great singer?

In business we have to work out what the true assets of the business are – what are our core strengths and abilities? What can we excel at? If we are great at marketing but very poor at administration, then we should probably stop spending time and energy trying to get our administrative systems fixed. We should outsource it to someone who is good at that and concentrate on playing the game we are good at – marketing.

Look for success stories, talk to delighted customers, ask them what makes your organization better than the others and then build on that. Find the right partners to compensate the areas where you are ordinary or weak and free up time to find creative new ways to exploit your strengths.

4. MAKE IT FUN

If you want your department to be creative, then make it a great place to have fun. Humour, playfulness and laughter go with creativity.

Innovation is a serious business but being serious does not help you get started. Humour involves challenging conventions, poking fun at taboos and coming up with the unexpected. For these reasons it is a natural companion for creativity.

Ask people how we could make the office more of a fun place to work and implement some of the best ideas.

Here are some things you could try:

- Hold a fancy dress party – try themes such as bad taste, loudest outfit, film stars, champions, animals, etc. Be wild but take care not to offend.

- Get volunteers to tell jokes at the start of a meeting.

- Have plenty of toys and creative materials like modelling dough and building bricks.

- Have games for break times – table football, pinball, darts, etc.

- Run icebreaker games and activities at the beginning of and during meetings.

- Go to an art shop and buy some artists' materials. Have an art workshop where people draw or sculpt for fun.

- Run an improvisation workshop where people are encouraged to try improvised comedy. It is great for breaking down inhibitions and for getting people out of their comfort zones.

When you run events where staff are encouraged to be silly or make fools of themselves it is best if the boss and other senior executives take the lead. By making fun of themselves they help break down barriers, debunk the hierarchy and empower others to be freethinking.

Google's mission statement claims that 'even the best technology can be improved' and 'innovation is in our bloodline'.

The company encourages staff to spend 20 per cent of their time on 'fun personal projects', an approach that has led to major innovations such as Google Earth, Froogle and Gmail.

Many of the best creativity exercises, such as Pass the Parcel (see page 87) are accompanied by laughter and hilarity as they encourage people to be bizarre. As they chortle and become more playful, people are more likely to come up with creative, unorthodox and radical solutions.

5. WELCOME FAILURE

Very often the best way to test an idea is not to analyse it but to try it. The organization that implements lots of ideas will most likely have many failures, but the chances are it will reap some mighty successes too. By trying numerous initiatives we improve our chances that one of them will be a star. As Tom Kelley of IDEO puts it, 'Fail often to succeed sooner.'

In an article in the *Financial Times*, published on 22 November 2006, Peter Aspden wrote about Deborah Bull, Artistic Director at the Royal Opera House in London. She is keen to encourage small companies of artists to come out with mad ideas and to try them. She says, 'We need to get away from the idea that everything has to be a hit at the box office and a hit with the critics. If everything we do succeeds, then we are failing, because if means we are not taking enough risks.'

Honda Motor Company entered the US market in 1959 with its range of low-powered motorcycles. It endured failure after failure as it learnt the hard way that little motorcycles popular in the Tokyo suburbs were not well received on the wide open roads of the USA. They eventually brought out a range of high powered bikes that became very popular. Soichiro Honda, the founder of Honda said, 'Many people dream of success. Success can only be achieved through repeated failure and introspection. Success represents the 1 per cent of your work that results from the 99 per cent that is called failure.'

What makes Silicon Valley so successful as the engine of high-tech growth? It is the Darwinian process of failure. Author Mike Malone puts it like this, 'Outsiders think of Silicon Valley as a success, but it is, in truth, a graveyard. Failure is Silicon Valley's greatest strength. Every failed product or enterprise is a lesson stored in the collective memory. We don't stigmatize failure; we admire it. Venture capitalists like to see a little failure in the résumés of entrepreneurs.'

To develop the concept of the benefits of failure, Penn State University has a course for engineering students called Failure 101. The students have to take risks and do experiments. The more failures they have, the sooner they can get an A grade!

Many great successes started out as failures. Columbus failed when he set out to find a new route to India. He found America instead (and because he thought it was India he called the natives Indians). Champagne was invented by a monk called Dom Perignon when a bottle of wine accidentally had a secondary fermentation. 3M invented glue that was a failure — it did not stick. But it became the basis for the Post-it® note, which was a huge success.

Daria Hazuda, Scientific Director for Merck, leads the team looking for drugs to combat HIV. In an article published in *Fortune* on 30 October 2006, she said, 'For me, a failed experiment is actually a rich source of information. People tend to focus on positive results. But if you look at people in the drug discovery businesses who are successful, it is often those who also learn from the negative. They take that information and synthesize it in a holistic way.'

Scientists at Pfizer tested a new drug called Viagra, to relieve high blood pressure. Men in the test group reported that it was a failure as regards high blood pressure but it had one beneficial side-effect. Pfizer, the manufacturers, investigated the side-effect and found that the drug had a dramatic effect on men's sexual vigour. Viagra became one of the most successful failures of all time.

Tips for succeeding through failure:

- Recognize and communicate that when you give people freedom to succeed, you give them freedom to fail too.

- Distinguish between two kinds of failure – honourable failure where an honest attempt at something new or different has been tried unsuccessfully, and incompetent failure where people fail for lack of effort or competence in standard operations.

- Make sure people know that honourable failures will not be criticized.

- Get people to admit to or even boast about failures they have had where they tried something innovative that did not succeed. Turn these into learning experiences.

■ In a culture that is very risk averse and keen to apportion blame tackle the issue head on by rewarding honourable failures. Publicly praise and reward those who have had them.

Even if the failure does not lead directly to a success, it can be seen as a step along the way. Edison's attitude to 'failure' is salutary. When asked why so many of his experiments failed he explained that they were not failures. Each time he had discovered a method that did not work.

Alessi is an Italian kitchenware company famous for its creative designs. It has a museum showcase of its most outstanding failures. Most companies' display cabinets feature their greatest successes but Alessi wants to remind its designers to avoid complacency and to see that failure is an important part of innovative achievement.

The innovative leader encourages a culture of experimentation. You must teach people that each failure is a step along the road to success. To be truly agile, you must give people the freedom to innovate, the freedom to experiment, the freedom to succeed. That means you must give them the freedom to fail too.

6. FEAR SUCCESS

Success can be an enemy of innovation. When thing are going well we can become blinded. Success becomes a prophylactic against disruptive ideas. Why should we change a winning formula? Don't mess with success! These are the sorts of things people say. And yet the business cemetery is littered with companies that were shooting stars – a brilliant success for a while, followed by an inexorable fall to earth. Gary Hamel says, 'Success breeds stewards, not entrepreneurs.' People want to conserve and nurture what they have. In this way business success can deter risk and entrepreneurial action.

Christensen (2003) gives cogent explanations for this process. He gives examples drawn from fields as varied as steel mills and disk drives. He shows that as new technologies come along, the leaders in the previous technologies fail to make the switch until it is too late. They make the classic mistake of listening to their customers! The customers tell them that they like their products and want bigger better, faster, slicker versions of the same. The leaders see the new technologies as risky and lower quality and they fear cannibalization of their mainstream revenues. Consequently it tends to be the newcomers who develop the new technologies and then eventually win over customers.

The political forces within the business tend to be inimical to new ideas. There is considerable revenue associated with the current successful model. Careers have been built on its growth. Any change to a new model threatens those revenues and those reputations.

The innovative leader has to vigorously fight the complacency of success. What is needed is a restless hunger for experimentation and change. The current success is temporary and a useful platform for the greater things ahead. We can only find those things by constantly testing new ways of doing things.

7. SET PUZZLES

Every business problem is a puzzle. So one way of preparing your people to become creative problem solvers is to practise with puzzles. Riddles, brainteasers, quizzes, logic problems, crosswords and party games are all good ice-breakers for your creative thinking sessions.

Lateral thinking puzzles (sometimes called situation puzzles) are good at developing questioning skills, listening, teamwork and imagination. They consist of strange situations where the team is given a limited amount of information and then has to ask questions in order to figure out what is going on. The quizmaster can answer questions with 'Yes', 'No' or 'Irrelevant'. Some examples are given in the box below – the answers are at the back of the book together with a list of recommended puzzle books (see page 188).

Psychic

You enter a parking lot and see a woman walking towards you. You then see a row of cars and immediately know which one is hers. How?

Jailbreak

A man planned his escape from prison very carefully. He could have escaped in the dead of night but he preferred to do it in the middle of the morning. Why?

The Deadly Drawing

A woman walked into a room and saw a new picture there. She immediately knew that someone had been killed. How?

These puzzles are taken from Sloane and MacHale (2000) *Super Lateral Thinking Puzzles*.

After you have practised with some of these puzzles try setting one of your current business issues in the form of a puzzle. Say, for example, that your issue is how to market a new form of toothbrush with a limited budget. You might phrase the problem as follows. 'A man found a way to get 1 million people to put something unusual into their mouths. What did he do?' Encourage people to ask questions, come at the problem from new directions and to generate many possible solutions – silly as well as rational.

8. USE THE RIGHT LANGUAGE

Let's say the challenge is to win an important bid. You say to your team, 'We must win this bid. We've got to do everything possible to win it.' You are commanding them and issuing an implied threat.

On the other hand you could say, 'We really want to win this bid. Let's think of every possible way we can succeed.' Now you are being inclusive and encouraging a positive, creative approach.

Words matter. The words that leaders choose in communicating will shape attitudes and behaviours. It is easy to fall into a macho style of talking based on a masculine, sporting and aggressive mentality. Directors say things like:

- 'We need to make our sales targets.'
- 'You should focus on the goals.'
- 'We've got to beat the competition.'
- 'We must work harder.'
- 'You ought to make more calls.'

All of these statements have an implied '... or else'. They all adopt the tone of a parent–child relationship where the leader is directing and exhorting the followers.

A small change in tone and style can bring about a big change in response. For example, you could try these sorts of messages:

- 'We want to beat our sales targets.'
- 'Let's work together to achieve these goals.'
- 'How can we delight our customers and differentiate ourselves from our competitors?'
- 'Let's talk about how we can be more effective.'
- 'We want to make the best use of our time by making more calls on the right people.'

Do you remember the brainstorm example in the section 'Redefine the problem?' Executives at a manufacturing plant were disappointed with the results when they asked shop floor workers the question, 'How can we improve productivity?' The same workers then produced a wealth of great productivity ideas when the question was changed to, 'How can we make your job easier?'

Choose words that are supportive, constructive and inspiring. Instead of giving instructions, pose questions that seek ideas and input. By doing so you can enthuse your people to be positive and creative.

9. MAKE YOUR OWN PRODUCTS OBSOLETE

The fear of 'cannibalization' has prevented many a promising idea. And yet it seems clear that if you do not cannibalize your own product line with better, cheaper, faster, more effective or more appealing products your competitors surely will.

US radio manufacturers dominated the radio market in the early 1950s. They knew about transistor technology but did not develop it as they did not want to threaten their high-quality and high-value valve-based radios. They disdained transistors as cheap and tinny with low power and low quality. The Japanese radio makers took advantage of this oversight to build better and better transistor radios and they eventually took the full market and wiped out the incumbent suppliers.

Nowadays things are different. A cross-disciplinary team of scientists at General Electric's (GE's) global research facility in Niskayuna, New York, was set the challenge of developing a new kind of electric lamp using an emerging technology called organic light-emitting diodes (OLEDs), most easily thought of as light-up plastic. Why? Call it creative destruction. That is what might be needed to save the iconic but struggling GE Lighting business. In a commodity business it was losing share to low-cost rivals. As outlined in an article in *Fast Company* published in August 2004, CEO Jeffrey Immelt responded by pushing to foster innovations that let GE widen its margins with hard-to-copy products rather than competing on incremental improvements and price.

If GE can cannibalize its light bulb business, then you can do the same with your products. Try new, lower cost and more appealing versions of your products or services. Experiment with new technologies and routes to market. Above all, instil an attitude that allows you to compete with, threaten and even make your leading lines obsolete – before somebody else does.

10. TRUST

Innovative leaders trust their people. They allow them to try out ideas. They empower their people to take initiatives.

In striving for an ideal behaviour it is sometimes useful to consider the opposite – the wrong behaviour. Control freak leaders do not trust their people. They micro-manage them. They tell them what to do. They discourage dissent. They do not welcome disruptive ideas or questioning of their commands. They fear failure and therefore they eschew risk. They are highly political and do not share ideas with other departments. They replace trust with control.

How can you build trust with your team? Start with a very frank dialogue. Ask what they want out of their job and how much freedom or supervision they think is ideal. Discuss goals rather than tasks and ends rather than means. Show that you are keen to help and support them. Stress that you want to be kept in the picture. Agree that within certain guidelines they can take action without asking you first. Always do what you say you will do. Be honest and treat people fairly. Be discreet. Admit your failings and apologize if you let your people down. Praise people for initiative and honest endeavour even if it results in failure.

Trust takes time to build and it can easily be destroyed. The good news is that most people are trustworthy and want to develop a trusting relationship. They are prepared to give you the chance to build that trust.

11. EMPOWER EMPLOYEES

Empowerment follows on from trust. Each one builds the other.

A young PhD in electronics, Ted Hoff, joined a start-up company in California in 1968. He was the 12th employee in a new venture called Intel. One of Intel's customers was a Japanese calculator manufacturer, Busicomp, who gave Intel the job of designing the electronic circuits for a new calculator. The job was given to Ted Hoff, who had never worked on calculator designs before. Busicomp had specified 12 hard-wired circuits to perform the 12 functions in the calculator. This looked very complicated to Hoff so he asked his boss if he could try a different approach. He wanted to experiment and see if he could develop one circuit that could do all 12 functions if it was programmed. His boss agreed – it was not what the customer had asked for but it was an interesting idea and Hoff's manager would cover for him if it did not work out. It did work out. Hoff invented the microprocessor. As a result of Hoff's imagination and his boss's trust, Intel had gained an innovation that would turbo-charge their growth into one of the most successful companies on the planet.

Dan Bricklin was working at Digital Equipment Corporation (DEC) in 1979 when he went to his boss with an idea for a software programme that could be used to manipulate numbers. His boss turned down the idea and told Bricklin to focus on meeting his current job objectives rather than experimenting with software projects. Bricklin quit his job in DEC in order to develop the idea, which he called the spreadsheet. He founded Visicorp Inc and launched the world's first spreadsheet, Visicalc. DEC had lost the spreadsheet.

What kind of a leader are you? Are you like Ted Hoff's boss who was supportive of Ted's radical idea and allowed him to pursue it? Or are you like Dan Bricklin's boss who was focused on delivering this quarter's goals and did not want anything distracting the team from achieving them?

Sir Richard Branson has a strong reputation as an innovative leader who empowers his people. At one famous staff meeting he asked if anyone had an idea for a business that Virgin should launch. An airline stewardess, Ailsa Petchey, ventured a suggestion. She was getting married soon and with her busy schedule had found difficulty in putting together all the things needed for her wedding. She recommended that Virgin put together a high-quality service to supply all the wedding items needed for the bride to be. Branson investigated the idea. He liked it and founded Virgin Bride. Then he asked Ailsa Petchey, who had proposed the idea, to head it up. She became the managing director of Virgin Bride. What sort of a message does that send to every other person who works at Virgin? Sir Richard Branson will back you and your idea. That is true empowerment.

Section 6:
Personal creativity

1. CHECK ASSUMPTIONS

We all make assumptions all the time. It would be impossible to get through life if we did not. We assume that the taxi driver knows his way and can drive. We assume that the chef in the restaurant will not poison us. We assume that the doctor is an expert and so we believe him or her.

But in business, assumptions are dangerous. Here are the sorts of assumptions we make:

- We cannot raise prices because of the competition.

- If we sell direct we will upset our channel partners.

- Old people are slow and inflexible; they would not fit in with our team.

- Customers expect excellent service.

- We should not try things that were tried and failed before.

- We cannot do it if it is not in the budget.

There are many examples of newcomers challenging the assumptions of established business leaders and winning:

- Anita Roddick challenged the assumption that cosmetics had to be in expensive bottles when the Body Shop launched its products in plastic containers.

- IKEA challenged the assumption that customers should not go into warehouses by getting customers to collect their furniture from the warehouse.

- The low-cost airlines like South-Western, Easyjet and Ryanair challenged the assumptions that you needed to issue tickets and sell through travel agents. Some would argue that they also challenged the assumption that customers want good service.

- Apple challenged the assumption that a personal computer was functional and not aesthetic.

- Amazon challenged the assumption that customers like to browse in bookstores before buying books.

The innovative leader knows that everyone in the organization needs to challenge assumptions. He or she has to show that the boundaries and limitations that we conform to are largely self-imposed. This is done using many of the methods and techniques given in this book. For example, the leader will:

- Tell stories about businesses that limited themselves because of their assumptions and were overtaken by freethinking upstarts.

- Run brainstorming sessions that encourage people to break the rules and to ask 'What if…?'

- Praise people who challenge conventional thinking.

- Set goals for people in terms of ends not means. Ask people to find their own route to the destination.

- Bring in outside thinkers, consultants and speakers to challenge internal orthodoxies.

- Hire the best, brightest and most daring candidates to fill key positions.

- Ask questions and encourage everyone else to do so.

2. ASK QUESTIONS

Small children are forever asking questions. They have an insatiable curiosity about the world around them. Sadly we lose that curiosity as we grow older. We accept things for what they are and we go with the flow.

Think back to the day you joined your organization – you would have asked many basic questions. Why do we do this? What is the purpose of this? Why don't we do it another way? And so on. After a while we stop asking those kinds of questions. We don't want to look foolish and we assume that we know the answers anyway.

Good disciplines to help you apply questions include Fishbone analysis, Why, Why? (see page 36) and Six Serving Men (see page 38). They all force you to ask multiple questions about situations.

Have you ever played the game where two people have a conversation that consists entirely of questions? Try playing it and then apply the same principles to your next business conversation. Make each thing you say a question; answer questions with constructive questions. In a dialogue the person asking questions is generally the one in control, the other is responding. When you ask a question you usually learn something from the answer. When you make a statement you learn nothing.

One of the biggest obstacles to creativity in the workplace is our tendency to find fault with other people's ideas. When someone comes out with a wacky idea we show how clever we are by shooting it down. Trevor Bayliss is the English inventor who first suggested the idea of a clockwork radio. People immediately criticized the idea. Radios were electric, so they had to contain batteries or mains connections. Why put in a large mechanical device to wind one up? It was a step backwards. No one would use it. It would be impractical. It would never catch on. And so on. Fortunately Bayliss persevered with his idea and the clockwork radio found a huge market in countries where people could not afford batteries but were quite content to wind up a radio every so often.

The next time someone comes to you with an idea that you can immediately find fault with don't criticize, ask questions. A great thing to say is, 'That sounds interesting, how would it work?' Keep asking questions about the idea. Build it up rather than point out problems. As you discuss the idea all sorts of possibilities occur. That is the power of questioning.

Innovative leaders have a restless curiosity. They know that there are always better ways to do things and they want to find them. They ask searching questions and they encourage their people to ask searching questions.

3. MOVE OUT OF YOUR COMFORT ZONE

This advice applies at the personal and the organizational levels. If you want to be more adventurous in your thinking, be more adventurous in your activities. Deliberately push yourself out of your routine. Try things you do not normally try. Do things that you have never done before. Do things that scare you. Most people operate in a comfortable rut. Here are some ideas for pushing you out of your rut:

- Take salsa dancing lessons
- Try a new sport.
- Drive a different route to work every day for a month.
- Learn to knit.
- Read some special interest magazines that you have never read before.
- Perform in a karaoke bar.
- Go to an art gallery.
- Go on a flower arranging course.
- Learn a foreign language.
- Join an amateur dramatic society and act a minor part in a play.
- Help in a charity shop.
- Become a prison visitor.
- Talk to somebody new every day. Listen to them carefully.

The same philosophy applies to your business. We tend to hide behind old mottos like:

- Stick to the knitting.
- Focus on your strengths.
- Don't try to be all things to all men.

These can be excuses for staying within our corporate comfort zone. It is by trying new activities that we gain new experiences and skills. If we keep doing the same things we learn very little.

Nokia was originally a small Finnish wood pulp company. Nokia diversified many times. The organization tried all sorts of different things. At one time it made rubber boots. Now it is one of the world's leading providers of mobile phones.

Virgin Group started as a record label. Richard Branson has led countless diversifications. Many experiments have failed, but they have established businesses in areas such as trains, airlines, books, cola, etc.

If we as individuals need a good push to get us out of our comfort zones, then unwieldy organizations need a mighty shove. It takes guts and determination to try new business initiatives in areas outside our core competence. This is what Lou Gerstner did when he turned around IBM. Gerstner was brought in as CEO to halt the slide as the giant corporation lumbered towards irrelevance and oblivion (see Gerstner, 2003). He took many deliberate and highly symbolic steps to change the company's culture and to turn it away from a dependence on products to become a leader in computer services.

4. SIMPLIFY THINGS

If you want to innovate around a process or service then try simplifying. Break the process down into all its component parts. Then next to each part write one of two words – essential or non-essential. When we say essential we mean absolutely essential; items that are highly desirable are still categorized as non-essential. Now we write a second and shorter list – just the essentials. We look at this and ask the question — how else could we achieve these essential actions? We can go further by looking at the non-essentials and asking – can we eliminate or replace any of these?

Say, for example, the process was selling a house. Our list of essential (E) and non-essential (NE) might look like this:

- Get valuations from estate agents.   NE
- Make urgent repairs.   NE
- Choose an estate agent.   NE
- Set the initial price.   NE
- Put the house on the market.   NE
- Advertise in local newspapers.   NE
- Tidy up, remove clutter.   NE
- Keep the house and garden neat.   NE
- Show prospective buyers around the house.   NE
- Find a buyer.   E
- Get the best price.   NE
- Exchange contracts.   E
- Handle any objections or survey issues.   NE
- Complete the sale.   E

The list of essential items is short – find a buyer, exchange contracts and complete the sale. We then ask is there a direct way to achieve this without all the other steps. How can we simplify the process to the shortest, most direct route to the goal? Do we need to go to estate agents or can we find a buyer direct – maybe through contacts or by using the internet? We then look at each of the desirable steps and challenge the necessity or method. It is easy to assume that the conventional method, the process that almost everyone uses, is the only way. But some people sell their homes via auction or lottery or direct on internet sites or at eBay. They all find a buyer, they all exchange contracts and they all complete the sale – they do the essentials – but they find other ways to get to them.

The major airlines had well-established and sophisticated processes for handling customers. Their processes had many steps including the following:

- Sell through travel agents.
- Issue tickets.
- Allocate seats.
- Check passengers in.
- Give a free hot drink to the customers on the flights.

When the low-cost carriers, such as South Western in the United States and Easyjet and Ryanair in Europe, looked at these processes they found that there was great scope for simplification. All of the above steps were found to be non-essential except for check the passengers in. And that step could be eliminated for passengers with hand luggage only. The low-cost carriers did not sell through travel agents but direct over the internet. They did not offer allocated seating. They did not give free hot drinks to passengers. They simplified the whole structure, reduced costs significantly and opened up a burgeoning new market for budget travel.

Focus on what is absolutely essential and try to conceive a novel and simple way of delivering it.

5. LOOK AT THINGS FROM A DIFFERENT ANGLE

Karen Brady became the Managing Director of Birmingham City Football Club at the age of 23. The club was in desperate straits but over the following 10 years she transformed it into a thriving and profitable premiership club. She succeeded largely because she took a different point of view from the men who tradition-ally run the game. She saw the club as an events company whose purpose was to maximize revenue from the performances. She applied new marketing methods to fill the ground and sell affinity products such as insurance to the fans.

Albert Szent-Gyorgy, who discovered Vitamin C, put it this way, 'Genius is seeing what everyone else sees and thinking what no one else has thought.' If you can survey a situation from a different viewpoint, then you have a good chance of gaining a new insight.

How can we force ourselves to take a different view of a situa-tion? We are so used to seeing an issue from one perspective that it is difficult to force ourselves. Instead of looking at the scene from your view, try looking at it from the perspective of a customer, a producer, a supplier, a child, an alien, a lunatic, a comedian, a dictator, an anarchist, an architect, Salvador Dali, Leonardo da Vinci and so on.

Lindsay Owen-Jones is the Englishman who, as CEO, brought a new perspective to the French group L'Oreal and has achieved remarkable growth. He was recently asked whether he feared new competition in cosmetics from Unilever and Procter & Gamble. He explained that L'Oreal has a different point of view from fast-moving consumer goods companies, 'Competition in our business is not about price wars and money-off coupons. The consumer is guided by product performance. Is it pleasur-able, seductive, imaginative and beautiful? Is this what I want at this moment in time?'

The great innovators did not take the traditional view and develop existing ideas. They took an entirely different view and transformed society. Picasso took a different view of painting,

Einstein imagined a new approach to physics, Darwin conceived a different view of creation. Each of them looked at the world in a new way. In similar fashion Jeff Bezos took a different view of book retailing with Amazon.com, Stelios took a new perspective on flying with Easyjet, Swatch transformed our view of watches and IKEA changed the way we buy furniture. If we can come at problems from entirely new directions, then we have unlimited possibilities for innovation.

6. TRUST YOUR INTUITION

MBA students are taught to treat business in a rational, scientific way. They analyse situations, develop financial models, critically examine management decisions and logically examine different scenarios. When they emerge from the hallowed halls of academia they are often surprised to find that businesses run much less on logic and much more on emotion. It is not cold, intelligent analysis that drives most organizations forward. Emotional energy is often the real engine behind successful people and organizations.

Sure it helps to be analytical, intelligent and rational, but what makes people like Richard Branson, Bill Gates or Steve Jobs great business leaders is not their undoubted intelligence but their passion and commitment to their cause.

One of the richest men in Britain is Felix Dennis, who made his fortune in publishing. In 1971 he was jailed for publishing an obscene political cartoon, but he was acquitted on appeal. His success started with *Kung-Fu Monthly* in 1974. In the 1980s he published a string of successful computer magazines. His publishing empire now spans IT, motoring, gambling and men's magazines. A recent innovation was *The Week* – a brief summary of all the best articles from the press each week. In his book, *How to Get Rich*, he describes how he ignores conventional wisdom and sound advice from his directors, lawyers and accountants. He goes with his gut instincts instead. As reported in an article by David Woodward in *Director Magazine*, published in September 2006, time and again Dennis trusted his intuition in making tough business decisions about innovative ventures.

Luc Mayrand, Concept Designer at Disney says, 'If you find your logic is talking you out of a good idea, question the logic first, then question the idea. This is entertainment; logic is less important than the impact of the story and design.'

There are many famous examples of where eminent people used logic and analysis to rubbish an innovative idea which subsequently succeeded. Western Union turned down the telephone because they saw no need for people to chat to one another. IBM turned down xerography when it was offered to them by its inventor Chester Carlson. Decca Records turned down the Beatles and so on.

Logic and analysis can always find fault with innovative ideas. Use these tools but use them warily. If your intuition tells you that you have a great idea, then pursue it a little while longer.

7. INCUBATE

One of the best ways for an individual to come up with great ideas is to incubate the problem. Do not look deliberately for ideas but follow this simple four step plan:

- Define the problem – as discussed above.

- Forget about it for a while. Do something else. Sleep on it.

- Wait for an idea or two suddenly to occur to you.

- Check out the ideas.

The critical part in this process is the second part, the incubation. It relies on the subconscious mind chewing the problem over in the background. Eventually something pops up.

James Webb Young describes the process this way, 'First the mind must gather its raw materials. Second the mind goes through a process of masticating those materials. You drop the whole subject and put it out of your mind. Then out of nowhere the idea will appear.'

Many great thinkers have used this technique. Try unleashing the power of your subconscious. You will be surprised at the results.

You can do this at an individual or group level. A leading US company brought its senior team to London. The key challenges facing them were described. Then the executives were told to walk around London and to visit the British Museum. In the late afternoon they reconvened to see what had been inspired. The change of environment and the variety of stimuli served to help generate fresh thinking and a multitude of ideas.

8. DON'T TAKE THE FIRST ANSWER

The macho manager is keen to be seen as decisive and can quickly come up with an idea for tackling most problems. Doing something is generally (but not always) a better option that doing nothing. But the first answer we come up with is unlikely to be the best answer.

A better approach is to take a little time to generate a long list of possible ideas and then evaluate them in order to select one or more to try. Our first idea is often the most obvious, the most straightforward response. It is rarely the best response. As we mull over the problem and force more and more possible solutions, we generate less conventional, less routine, less automatic choices – we come up with the creative, the radical and the better options.

When men first wanted to fly, the most obvious way to do it was to copy birds by beating two large wings against the air. This was tried and failed many times. But people kept on trying it. In the year the Wright brothers first flew, the US Congress voted to stop funding heavier-than-air flying experiments because they were such an obvious waste of time and money. The aerofoil wing section, which gives lift when driven forward, was a very different and much better option than flapping wings.

When you find yourself tempted to rush into a quick answer, force yourself to pause for a moment. Would it be better to get the opinions of others? Should you run a short brainstorm meeting? Should you ponder the issue yourself for a while? Could you write down several different approaches rather than just one? Some problems demand an immmediate response but many do not; they favour a more considered approach. The first idea you come up with may be great, but the chances are that the tenth, twentieth or fortieth idea will be much better.

9. DEVELOP YOUR PERSONAL CREATIVITY

It is easy to think that brainstorming and idea generation is a group activity. Many great ideas come from group sessions. But even more come from individuals.

Most of the principles we have looked at in this book apply at an individual level too. In particular you should:

- Set personal innovation goals.
- Allocate time for reflection.
- Challenge your personal assumptions and self-limiting beliefs.
- Look for stimulation from new sources.
- Mix with different people and ask them for their ideas and opinions.
- Keep asking questions, listening and learning.
- Be positive about risk and personal failures.

When you have a tough problem, try talking it over with someone who has nothing to do with the situation. He or she will often ask basic questions or make seemingly silly suggestions that prompt good ideas. Two heads are better than one, but people who are too close to the issue will often come up with the same ideas as you, so try an outsider.

Ask how some celebrity would tackle the issue – what would Steve Jobs do? Or Bob Geldof, or Richard Branson, or Salvador Dali or Margaret Thatcher or Madonna or Sherlock Holmes? Take each individual's approach to its extremes and it will likely give you some radical solutions.

In addition here is one important tip for personal creativity. Always carry an ideas notebook with you. Whenever you see something interesting or have a good idea make a note of it. It is easy to lose good ideas. They are like butterflies – beautiful and intriguing for an instant and then they flutter away and are forgotten. Make sure that you capture your thoughts in the notebook. You can write challenge headings on different pages. Beneath write questions or concepts. Draw mind maps of problems. Keep pages for random jottings.

10. BECOME AN EVANGELIST

It is all very well for company directors and business leaders to have grandiose plans for innovation but what if you are in the middle or lower reaches of an organization? How can you initiate change? Are you powerless to drive innovation? It can often feel that way. It can be very hard for the people at the top to change the direction of the supertanker, so what chance do the cabin staff have?

Middle-ranking managers and staff members can help their companies to become more innovative, though no one would claim it is easy. If you are in this position and you see a great opportunity that you are convinced the company should pursue, you must build a lobby of support for the idea.

Hamel (2002) gives examples of people who have done this. In 1994 John Patrick and David Grossman were determined to galvanize the lumbering giant IBM into a nimble response to the opportunity of the internet. Initially IBM, with its investment in mainframe computers and corporate systems, failed to see that the internet was going to revolutionize their world. In this respect they were in good company – even Microsoft overlooked the importance of the internet at first. Patrick and Grossman saw that here was a trend that their employers could not afford to miss, so they launched a subversive internal campaign. They found a network of enthusiasts and activists. They launched a 'manifesto' and circulated it by e-mail. They gave demonstrations of the internet's capabilities to senior executives. They took risks, broke the rules and exceeded their authority. Eventually their pleas were heard, they turned around the supertanker and IBM became a leader in e-commerce and web services.

If you are in this position of wanting to encourage a specific innovation and trying to influence those above and around you here are some tips:

- Build a coalition of the like-minded.
- Lobby at the very highest levels.
- Gain a high-level sponsor as soon as you can.

- Gather data, trends and external evidence that support your case.

- Start small. Establish some small successes – a trial or a prototype that customers like.

- Be prepared to take risks and break some rules.

If your cause is a good one, then it is likely to be recognized as such. There is a risk that you will be seen as a trouble maker in your organization and that will damage your career – but if that is the case do you want to work there anyway? It is more likely that you will be surprised. You will find that the senior team welcome someone with the initiative, insight and passion to change the organization. Constructive rebels are needed in every business and leaders know this.

11. SIMPLIFY YOUR LIFE

The number one obstacle to innovation is time. Many people are just too busy to find time for creative activity. People have too much going on and too much complexity in their lives already. They have little appetite for trying new things. If this is your problem here is some advice from writer Elaine St James:

- Resign from any organizations whose meetings you dread.

- Learn to live with less information: stop watching TV news, cancel half your magazine subscriptions.

- Work where you live, or live where you work.

- Be in bed by 9.00 pm one night a week.

- Live on half of what you earn, save the other half.

- Keep asking 'Is this going to simplify my life?'

To which we can add some more:

- Make a 'stop doing' list of things you do regularly but don't need to do.

- Stop reading gloom-ridden newspaper reports, stop speaking to negative, cynical people.

- Simplify finances by reducing the number of accounts, standing orders, direct debits, credit cards, insurances and investments you have. Consolidate and save time.

- Delegate more.

The Pareto Principle tells us that 80 per cent of the benefit of our actions comes from 20 per cent of what we do. The other 80 per cent of what we do is of low value. Let's eliminate the least value activities.

If we can de-clutter our lives, we can free time for important things. Look at your garage or your study – are they filled with junk that never gets used? Is your life in a similar state? If you can eliminate the junk in your garage or the pile of papers that are never read in your study, then you can take a similar approach to all the time drainers in your life.

12. BE DISCONNECTED

The modern tendency is to be always connected and always in contact. Mobile phone, e-mail and BlackBerry or PDA equipment mean that we are forever in touch. Many of these contacts are not crucial or even necessary. They just make us feel important and involved. The downside is that they curtail our free thinking time.

Bill Gross, the Chief Investment Officer of Pimco, manages a portfolio worth some US $200 billion. He says:

> I don't have a cellphone, I don't have a BlackBerry. My motto is, I don't want to be connected – I want to be disconnected. The most important part of my day isn't on the trading floor. Every day at 8:30 am, I get up from my desk and walk across to a health club across the street. I do yoga and work out for probably an hour and a half, between 8:30 am and 10. ... After about 45 minutes riding the exercise bike and maybe 10 or 15 minutes of yoga, all of a sudden some significant light bulbs seem to turn on. I look at that hour and a half as the most valuable time of the day. (Taken from an article entitled 'Secrets of success' published in *Fortune* magazine on 20 March 2006).

A writer found that when his internet connection was disconnected for a week his productivity shot up. He wrote more in that week than in any other month of the year.

Most of us need some time alone to quietly reflect on key issues. If we are constantly in communication with people, we deny ourselves the opportunity for serious thought. Try giving yourself a quiet period each day and using it to mull over important points. Get disconnected!

13. VISUALIZE WITH MIND MAPS

Many people find that mind maps are a great aid to personal creativity. Mind maps can be used for a variety of purposes including note taking, problem analysis and simply for recording ideas.

This is how Buzan, the originator of the concept, describes the mind map process for creativity (Buzan, 1977):

In the centre of a page draw an image of the thing around which you want to generate creative ideas.

Working with speed uppermost in your mind, branch off from the centre, connecting ideas wherever they fit in as fast as they come into your head. When doing this, it is best to keep a single word per line, as each word has its own massive series of associations, and if kept separate will tend to spark off more ideas and images than it will do if trapped in a phrase or sentence. Images and words on the branches near the centre are usually the primary ideas. And the secondary and dependent ideas branch towards the boundary of your pattern. Sometimes, however, you will notice that an idea or image pops up all over the place at the extremes, and because of this omnipresence, you will realise that it is perhaps the underlying concept with which you are really concerned.

Below is an example taken from Buzan's website: www.buzan-world.com.

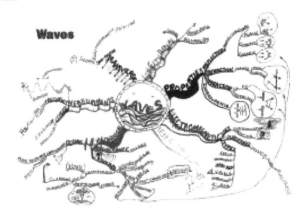

Figure 4

14. KEEP FIT

A flabby lifestyle can lead to flabby attitudes and flabby thinking. To have an active, creative brain it is important to have an active lifestyle. That means the right diet and the right level of fitness. There are many self-help books on these subjects. Here is a summary of the top advice:

- Cut out junk food.

- Reduce caffeine and coffee intake.

- Reduce alcohol intake.

- Cut out fatty foods.

- Cut out pre-prepared foods.

- Eat more vegetables.

- Eat more fruit.

- Drink plenty of water.

- Get a pedometer to measure your steps.

- Walk 10,000 steps a day.

- Walk or cycle instead of taking the car on short journeys.

- Take up tennis, golf, squash or some other active sport.

- Run.

- Swim.

- Get enough sleep – seven hours a night minimum.

- Relax, take time out from stress.

Sitting in the same place for most of the day is bad for the body and it does little to stimulate the mind. On the other hand, a hectic day where you are dashing from one busy activity to the next is stressful and gives you little time to think. There is a balance that has to be struck. Plan to give yourself some time each day for exercise and some time for relaxation and quiet reflection. Some people find that they have their best ideas while walking to work or on a running machine at the gym (see 'Be disconnected' on page 180). If it works for you, take a dictation machine with you and record your thoughts.

15. BE LUCKY

It might seem a strange piece of advice – be lucky. But there is more to it. Dr Richard Wiseman has studied why some people are lucky and some are not. He advises (Wiseman, 2004) that there are four main traits that lucky people have that help them to be 'lucky':

- They create, notice, and act upon chance opportunities that come up.

- They make good decisions using their intuition as well as their logic.

- They have positive expectations about the future.

- They don't let bad luck get them down; they find a way to turn it into good fortune.

By changing your attitudes, behaviours and actions you can change your luck. This is well established and is familiar territory for readers of self-help books. But it is worth reiterating in the contexts of creativity and innovation. Creativity involves pushing the boundaries and moving out of your comfort zone. Innovation entails trying experiments and undertaking risk. Both will mean failures along the way.

Many people blame bad luck for their failures – especially on ventures where they invested considerable time and effort. People with a positive outlook recognize that each obstacle is a step along the way and that there is much that can be learnt from setbacks. They learn lessons from reverses and they seek out fresh opportunities. They are always optimistic and receptive to ideas. They see opportunities in situations where others give up. They make their own good luck. So be lucky!

Conclusion

Innovative leaders have a vision for change in the business, they develop a culture for innovation and they implement processes for innovation. The vision is an overarching statement of what the organization stands for and what it intends to achieve. It is a clear and ambitious goal, which is inspiring but believable. From this goal are derived the strategy, objectives and metrics for innovation.

The leader cultivates a culture that is open, questioning and listening. Fear of failure and fear of the unknown are overcome with an atmosphere that encourages experimentation. There is no blame for honest trials that do not succeed. People are trusted and empowered to try new ways of doing their job. There is a positive attitude towards risk management.

A clear vision and a supportive culture are essential for an innovative organization, but they are not sufficient. In addition we need processes. These processes focus on the generation, evaluation, selection and implementation of ideas. The purpose is to fill and manage a pipeline of innovation projects. Typically this starts with a highly effective employee suggestions scheme. Ideas are encouraged from a variety of sources – internal and external. There is an urgency about selecting and implementing the best ideas – they have to pass hurdles but they are not subjected to inappropriate tests or undue delays. The leader is happy to see a large quantity of ideas going into the pipeline and significant numbers making it through to trials and prototypes.

He or she is quick to encourage the testing of new ideas and yet quite relaxed about killing off the ideas that are clearly not working (despite the sunk cost). At all stages there are measures in place to ensure that the innovation pipeline is healthy. Key metrics involve numbers of ideas at each stage and the time it takes to get from concept to implementation.

Typically the innovative leader is both analytical and creative. Although they contribute significantly to the process, innovative leaders recognize that the key is not their own abilities – it lies in enabling the creative talents of their teams. They do not promote themselves or claim credit for success but are quick to recognize and reward the ideas and entrepreneurial activities of others. Innovative leaders find great ways to inspire their people to achieve extraordinary results and to exceed expectations. They attract and retain great teams. They cope with change by driving it. They use innovation as a tool to change the world.

References and further reading

Ackoff, R L, Magidson, J and Addison, H J (2006) *Idealized Design*, Wharton School Publishing, University of Pennsylvania

Allan, D, Kingdon, M, Murrin, K and Rudkin, D (1999) *What if!*, Capstone Publishing, Oxford

Boston Consultancy Group (2006) *Measuring Innovation*, www.bcg.com

Buzan, T (1977) *Make the Most of your Mind*, Pan, London

Christensen, C (2003) *The Innovator's Dilemma*, HarperCollins, New York

Collins, J (2001) *Good to Great*, Random House, London

de Bono, E (2000) *Six Thinking Hats*, Penguin, Harmondsworth

Dennis, F (2006) *How to Get Rich*, Ebury Press, London

Drucker, P (1993) *Innovation and Entrepreneurship*, Butterworth Heinemann, Oxford

Gerstner, L (2003) *Who says Elephants Can't Dance?* Harper-Collins, London

Hamel, G (2002) *Leading the Revolution*, Harvard Business School Press, Cambridge, Mass.

Kelley, T (2002) *The Art of Innovation*, HarperCollins Business, London

National Audit Office (2006) *Achieving Innovation in Central Government Organizations*, July 2006, London

Sloane, P (2003) *The Leader's Guide to Lateral Thinking Skill*, Kogan Page, London

Sloane, P *How to Generate Ideas*, www.destination-innovation. com

Tucker, R (2002) *Driving Growth through Innovation*, Barrett-Koehler, California

Wiseman R (2004) *The Luck Factor*, Arrow, London

Wolff, J (2001) *Do Something Different*, Virgin Books, London

Puzzle answers

PSYCHIC

The woman is carrying a kettle. It is a frosty morning and only one of the cars has the windshield de-iced. You deduce that she defrosted her windscreen and is returning the kettle.

JAILBREAK

The man knew that his escape would be detected in about half an hour. He timed it at 10.30 am on a Tuesday – just 30 minutes before the regular weekly alarm test, when everyone in the surrounding area would ignore the siren.

THE DEADLY DRAWING

She entered the room and saw the chalk picture outline of a body on the floor. It was the site of a recent murder and the chalk marked the position of the body.

These puzzles are taken from Sloane, P and MacHale, D (2000) *Super Lateral Thinking Puzzles*, Sterling Publishing.

Also recommended are:

Sloane, P (1991) Lateral Thinking Puzzlers

Sloane, P and MacHale, D (1993) *Challenging Lateral Thinking Puzzles*

Sloane, P and MacHale, D (1994) *Great Lateral Thinking Puzzles*

Sloane, P and MacHale, D (2006) *Cunning Lateral Thinking Puzzles*

All published by Sterling Publishing, New York

Index